Coding For Kids 8-12

2 Books In 1 - Scratch 3.0 And Python

The Most Complete Programming Book For Toddlers Full Of Fun Theory And Challenging Exercises With Solutions (Includes Step By Step Guides)

© Copyright 2020 by Raymond Deep - All rights reserved.

This eBook is provided with the sole purpose of providing relevant information on a specific topic for which every reasonable effort has been made to ensure that it is both accurate and reasonable. Nevertheless, by purchasing this eBook, you consent to the fact that the author, as well as the publisher, are in no way experts on the topics contained herein, regardless of any claims as such that may be made within. As such, any suggestions or recommendations that are made within are done so purely for entertainment value. It is recommended that you always consult a professional prior to undertaking any of the advice or techniques discussed within.

This is a legally binding declaration that is considered both valid and fair by the Committee of Publishers Association and the American Bar Association and should be considered as legally binding within the United States.

The reproduction, transmission, and duplication of any of the content found herein, including any specific or extended information, will be done as an illegal act regardless of the end form the information ultimately takes. This includes copied versions of the work, both physical, digital, and audio unless express consent of the Publisher is provided beforehand. Any additional rights reserved.

Furthermore, the information that can be found within the pages described forthwith shall be considered both accurate and truthful when it comes to the recounting of facts. As such, any use, correct or incorrect, of the provided information will render the Publisher free of responsibility as to the actions taken outside of their direct purview. Regardless, there are zero scenarios where the original author or the Publisher can be deemed liable in any fashion for any damages or hardships that may result from any of the information discussed herein.

Additionally, the information in the following pages is intended only for informational purposes and should thus be thought of as universal. As befitting its nature, it is presented without assurance regarding its prolonged validity or interim quality. Trademarks that are mentioned are done without written consent and can in no way be considered an endorsement from the trademark holder.

Table of Contents

Book 1: Coding for Kids - Scratch 3.0

Introduction 1

Chapter 1 Meet Scratch 3 – Your New Digital Friend 3

Chapter 2 Exploring Scratch 10

Chapter 3 Bad to the Code – Learning skills for life 15

Chapter 4 Keeping Your Cool While You Code 20

Chapter 5 Coding Tips and Tricks 47

Chapter 6 Creating a Plan for Your Project 55

Chapter 7 What Coding Can Do for You 61

    Reasons to Code 62

    Coding Is Used Nearly Everywhere 63

    Coding Can Make You Smarter and Improve Your Self-Confidence 63

    You Don't Need to Be A Programmer to Benefit 66

    Coding as a Career 68

    Machine Learning and Data Science 71

    Training to Code 72

Building Your Skills Over Time 74

Learning to Build a Toolbox 75

Chapter 8 Activities and Games.. 78

Chapter 9 25 guided activities 107

Chapter 10 Programming Languages and Tools to Learn............. 109

High-Level vs. Low-Level Languages 109

The First Computer Languages 111

Computer Syntax 113

Logic Errors 114

Programming Mobile/Smart Phones 114

What Is a Compiler? 116

Interpreters... 117

Debugging 118

Higher Level Tools 119

High-Level Tools for Video Games 120

Language Tools Everyone Should Know 123

Career options 125

Conclusion 130

Introduction 134

Book 2: Python For Kids

Chapter 1 What is Coding? 140

    Why do you need to code your resources? 141

    Programming languages 143

    Compilers and interpreters 147

    What can you make with code? 150

Chapter 2 Python Theory 153

    Artificial Intelligence 154

    Machine Learning 155

    Deep Learning 159

Chapter 3 Welcome to Python! 162

    The Best Starting Point 164

Chapter 4 Step-by-step and must know 171

    On a pc 171

    On Mac 175

    Using idle 179

    Saying hi to python! 182

    Saving your work 183

Running a program 188

Chapter 5 Python Data Types **192**

    Numbers 193

    Sequences 194

    Sets 197

    Mappings 199

    Boolean 200

    Mutable vs Immutable data types 200

    Chapter exercises 201

Chapter 6 Variables and Operators **204**

    Variables 204

    Operators 207

    Combining Operators 211

Chapter 7 Python Strings **213**

    Accessing Characters in a String 214

    String Slicing 216

    String Methods 217

    Check String 219

    String Formatting Operator (%) 221

Unicode String 222

Chapter 8 Loops 224

Pseudocode 225

While Loops 228

Increment and Decrement 234

Generating Random Numbers 236

Chapter 9 For Loop 240

Nested loops 242

Nested for loop 242

Nested While loop 243

Control Statements 245

Pass 250

Arrays 251

Access an array 254

Append() method 255

Insert value in an array 256

Extend an array 256

pop() method 259

Reverse an array 260

viii

Chapter 10 IF, statement 262

    Comparing Variables 262

    Elif and Or 268

    Chapter Game! 271

    Nesting Ifs and Loops 272

Chapter 11 Turtle 274

Chapter 12 Fun Activities 284

    Activity 1: How old are you? 284

    Activity 2: Cookie Comparison 285

    Activity 3: Pie Party! 288

    Activity 4: Outfit Checker 290

    Activity 5: Logical Lab 293

    Activity 6: Planetary Exponentiation 296

    Activity 7 : Finding the sum of 1 + 2 + 3 + … + 100 297

    Activity 8: Finding the product of 2 × 4 × 6 × 8 × 10 299

    Activity 9: Finding the average value of positive numbers 301

    Activity 10: Counting the numbers according to which is greater 302

    Activity 11: Counting the numbers according to their digits 303

    Activity 12: How many numbers fit in a sum 304

Activity 13: Iterating as many times as the user wants 306

Activity 14: Rice on a chessboard 307

Activity 15: Find the secret number 309

Chapter 13 Learning Games 312

Rock Paper scissors 312

Guessing Game 317

Choose a Card 321

Chapter 14 Advance Games 326

Creating Your Skier Game 326

Creating a Tic-Tac-Toe Game 334

Launching a ball at a random angle 344

Conclusion: 354

Coding For Kids Scratch 3

A Step By Step Visual Guide For Beginners To Learn How To Code With Guided Activities And Build Your Own Computer Games (Includes 25 Coding Challenges With Keys)

Introduction

Congratulations on downloading *Coding for Kids,* and thank you for doing so. The following chapters will discuss helpful coding techniques for children. As technology becomes more integrated into our society, it is essential that we as people progress with it.

But the question is, how do we do such a thing? The answer lies in our children, who, unlike us, are being born into an age in which everything is in reach with the advancement of the modern world. Because of this, it's extremely important that we not only teach our children how to survive in this new world but thrive in it.

Coding is not only a valuable ability to have but an engaging activity that helps promote creativity, develop problem-solving skills and can give them a head start in a respected career. Parents can provide guidance and support throughout this process that will not only aid in the child's growth but establish a connection that bonds them emotionally and intellectually. Critical thinking skills and learning how to solve problems are important skills that are going to be needed in the 21st century. There are many career paths that are going to be open to those that have these kinds of skills, and coding is a great way to help build them. Even if a child does not go on to coding as a career choice, the experience of learning to code will help them in whatever endeavors they become involved with.

Scratch, a kid-oriented coding website provides users with the basic building blocks they need to properly introduce them into the domain of coding without overwhelming them. The simplicity of this website allows children to construct a necessary knowledge and understanding that permits growth later in life in regard to coding.

There are plenty of books on coding for children on the market, thanks again for choosing this one! Every effort was made to ensure it is full of as much useful information as possible. Please enjoy!

Chapter 1

Meet Scratch 3 – Your New Digital Friend

Have you ever wanted to make your own computer games? What about your own animated movies starring characters you created? Adventure stories that you can share with all of your friends and family? All of this is easy to do if you know how and have the tools to do it with. You may think it might be hard making all of these things on your own, but with this book, you can learn how to make them all yourself!

With the help of Scratch, you can create your own world of wonder. This book will teach you the basics of coding through the Scratch website and even includes activities that you can do all by yourself. Scratch is a website made especially for kids that makes coding both easy and fun. There is even a community of other users on Scratch where you can see their creations, they can see yours, and you can even work together on projects! With your parents' help, you can sign up for Scratch, start coding, and let your imagination fly.

How to sign up for Scratch

Signing up for Scratch is very simple to do, and after you sign up, you'll get to use the tools on the site to bring all of your dreams to life! Before you sign up, it's really important that you ask for your parent's permission. The internet is a big place, and it's really easy to get lost or get into trouble.

Step 1: First, go to https://scratch.mit.edu. There should be 2 options at the top that say, 'Join Scratch' or 'Sign In.' Because this is your first time on Scratch, you should click 'Join Scratch' to sign up. Whenever you want to come back to work on a project on Scratch, click on 'Sign In' using the username and password that you chose when joining Scratch.

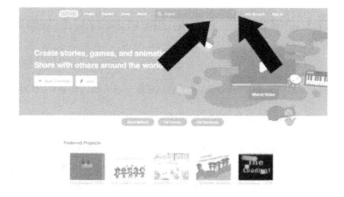

Step 2: After clicking 'Join Scratch,' you'll be asked to make your own username and password. Don't make your username your real name! Choose something special that shows other people on Scratch what you're all about. For example, if you absolutely LOVE cupcakes, it could be something like 'CupcakeLover3000' or 'CoolCupcakeCat.' It can be anything that you want as long as it's not unkind, horrible, or inappropriate. When choosing a password, make sure it's easy for you to remember but hard for others to guess. If you need help remembering, ask one of your parents to write it down for you and keep it somewhere safe.

Step 3: Next, you'll be asked things about your birthday, gender, and the country you live in. The answers that you provide here will help make your experience on Scratch customized to your exact needs and wants, depending on this information.

Step 4: You'll need your parents' help with this step. Ask them to enter their email address to confirm your account that way; you can begin commenting and sharing your projects with other members of the Scratch.

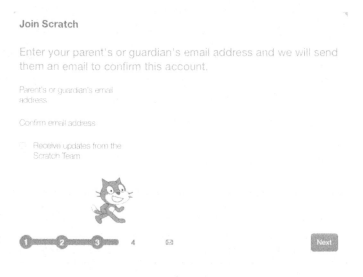

Step 5: The next page will confirm your new Scratch account and an email sent to your parents that will help you activate all the features to begin making friends and creating your own content using Scratch's tools.

Join Scratch

Welcome to Scratch, loserbutt!

You're now logged in! You can start exploring and creating projects.

If you want to share and comment, simply click the link in the email we sent you at **mymorton1@catamount.wcu.edu**.

Wrong email? Change your email address in Account Settings.

Having problems? Please give us feedback.

Now that you have a Scratch Account

Even though the goal of this website is to express yourself and have fun, having a Scratch account is a big responsibility that you must be aware of. The Scratch community is made up of other kids like yourself, teachers, and parents who deserve to be treated with respect and kindness. Even though this is an online website where you probably won't see these people face to face, think of it as a school. A school is a place where you come to learn, make friends, and enjoy yourself. Like at a school, people can see what you're doing on Scratch. The way you act online is how people will see you. You don't want to look mean or nasty, do you? Or you wouldn't want someone being mean or nasty to you, right? Scratch like a school has rules to make sure that it is a welcoming and friendly space for everyone. These are called community guidelines. Everyone who joins Scratch must follow these.

Community Guidelines

Everyone who contributes on Scratch needs to:

- **Be respectful.** This means when you share your projects or post comments on other people's projects, remember that kids of many different ages – some may even be younger than you - can see what you've shared.
- **Be constructive.** When making comments on other's projects, say something you like about it and tell them what you think they could do next time.
- **Share.** It's okay to remix projects, images, ideas, or anything you find on Scratch – and anyone can do the same with anything that you create. Make sure to give the other person credit when you remix.
- **Keep personal info private.** To keep everyone on Scratch safe, don't use your real names, anyone else's name, or post contact information like phone numbers, addresses, or anything that could put you or someone else in danger.

- **Be honest.** Don't pretend to be other Scratchers, tell stories that aren't true, or try to fool the community into thinking that you're someone that you're not.
- **Help keep the site friendly.** If you think a project that someone made or that a comment that someone posted is mean, rude, or causing harm to someone else or yourself, you should tell the Scratch team about it. By clicking "Report," you can let the Scratch team know about it and solve the problem. No bullies are allowed on Scratch!

Chapter 2

Exploring Scratch

Now that your account has been made, you can begin diving into the wonderful world of Scratch! The home page features a few different features that encourage you to begin creating and coding easily to get the ball rolling on your own projects. The homepage can get you connected with other Scratch users, give you the latest news about the site, and introduce you to studios and projects that you can work with to make unique projects or remix already existing works.

Following other users can inspire you to think outside of the box, stray from your comfort zone and appreciate how others think. This will help you not only grow as a coder, a creator but as a person too. Communicating with different people of different backgrounds and then seeing what they have to offer in creative projects and their own unique opinions can bring people closer together. This can help you gain a better understanding of the world and the people in it.

Featured Projects

Exploring the featured projects and studios on the homepage can also help other Scratchers gain popularity and promote collaborations, which can bring about more magnificent opportunities for you and for them. The Scratch community is very much like a family, families uplift each other, help members of the family work towards success, and encourage them to be better. By viewing their projects, giving feedback, and inspiring others by making your own content, you can strengthen the bond of you and others on the site and make beautiful connections between you and other users.

Curated Projects

Every week a different Scratch user is chosen to pick their favorite projects to be shown on the Scratch homepage. All you need to do is send in an application made up of an original project and a sample studio. After you've finished your application, post a link to your project in the comments section of the studio. Click on Learn More to access more information about the application and the process of becoming a curator!

Scratch Design Studio

A different design studio is featured on the homepage every month with a different theme to stimulate your artistic juices and make your dreams a reality! The studio offers advice and ideas on how to get started and showcases other users' work so you can either base your work on theirs or go a completely different direction with it! The choice is yours to make.

Remixing

Remixing is another activity that is popular among other Scratch users. If you have any original characters that you like to draw or animate, there are people that find joy in redrawing your characters and put their own personal twists on them. This can be useful for you because it can help you develop these characters more and further their stories so that their final form can be finished. This is also good for the remixers because they are able to perfect their drawing skills and completely reimagine an idea that was shown to them. Other remixing requests may ask you to add to animation or rework a game that somebody has made. This can help you become familiar with the different types of projects that you can do on Scratch. The basics of the project are already there; you just go on and remix to your heart's content! There are so many different projects to remix, and so many people who want to remix your own creations. It's a win-win for everyone.

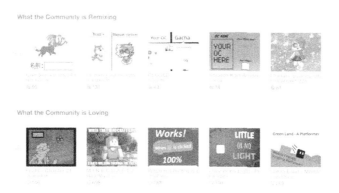

What the community is loving

If you've ever been on YouTube, then you know what the trending page is. What the community is loving' is similar to that. All of the projects that are gaining popularity throughout Scratch will be featured here. Some people make full-length comics, engaging games, funny memes, or animated shorts that you can view and share along with other Scratch users. Your new projects could be featured here! This is a great honor because it means that people are viewing your work, appreciating it, and becoming inspired to remix or create their own works. Being on the 'What the community is loving' tab can help you because users may give feedback that can help you become a better creator and help build your skills on Scratch.

Chapter 3

Bad to the Code – Learning skills for life

Now we'll be moving on to the nitty-gritty work! Coding and creating. Don't worry, though; there's nothing to be afraid of. This guide will explain all the things you need to know in order to start creating your own projects in a way that is simple and easy for you to understand. Typical coding for adults is WAY more challenging and complex, which, if you want to do when you get older, it's best to learn the basic techniques now to get your feet wet and introduce you to the process before diving straight in. Coding is a really valuable skill for you to have and can do a lot of good for you and others if you choose to continue coding.

During this process, it's important to not be afraid to ask for help. Whether it be from a parent, a teacher, or a close friend, asking for help is one of the most important steps in learning. Everyone has trouble from time to time, and if something doesn't work the first time for you, it's good to try again to figure it out for yourself and then ask for help. Don't ever give up if it seems too hard or if you don't get it quite right. No one is perfect their first try at anything, so just stick with it and you can become the coder you've always wanted to be.

Without further ado, let's jump into the colorful and captivating world of coding!

On the homepage, you will notice one of the tabs says 'Create.' I'll explain the other tabs later, but the 'Create' tab is the one that you will no doubt use the most on Scratch and, no doubt, the most important. This tab will take you to your own private creator studio, where you can begin making your own original work and pieces. This is going to be your own little spot in the world where you're free to create what you want how you want without fear of people making fun of you or judging you.

Language

By clicking on the globe, you can change the language to the one that you feel most comfortable with or the one that you speak comfortably. There are many languages to choose from, so you don't have to settle for one just because it's what everyone speaks. If you click on the file, there are multiple options to keep you organized and to keep your files secure, so you don't lose them.

File tab

Save now allows you to save your project so that you can go back and work on it later if you haven't finished it or would just like to work on it later. Save as a copy lets you save the project as a copy so that you can have multiple copies of the same work, so you don't have to worry about losing them or accidentally deleting them. There is another option to save it to your computer so that you can have a copy on your computer in case something goes wrong, and the copy that you have saved on Scratch messes up. If that happens, you can now load this file from your computer just as you would on the website! It's a very smart idea for a coder to have multiple copies of their work in the event that something happens because then you can have another way of getting to your project rather then it being lost forever. Sometimes there are little hiccups in life, whether it be a poor internet connection, a faulty computer, or an annoying little brother or sister that insists that they want to help that may put your work at risk of being deleted. Saving multiple copies in multiple places is a very responsible thing that you can do to save you a lot of time, effort, and heartache.

Code tab

We'll start with the basics of how to find your way around the design studio and begin your journey on Scratch. If you click on the Code tab, you will see that there are many different aspects of the coding process that you can use in whatever way you like in order to get your project to function in your special style. These aspects control the movement, the design, and sound, which you can combine and alter to your liking to not only make your work come to life but ensure that it is of the utmost quality. Scratch makes coding especially stress-free with its drag and drop feature. Do you see those little blocks in the screenshot below? Each of these little blocks has commands on them that tell your sprite what it needs to do in the way that you tell it to. You can switch the order of these factors so that they perform in a variety of ways to help you perfect your work or create something unique that you can be proud of.

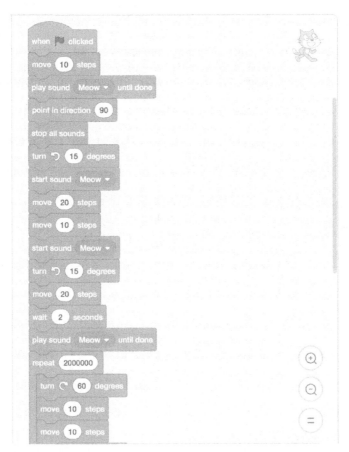

Chapter 4

Keeping Your Cool While You Code

Scratch is only scratching the surface of what the world of coding can offer you. Once you learn the basic building blocks, you can easily learn advanced coding skills when you get older, which you can use to build your own websites, develop your own full-length computer games, or make your own phone apps. If you enjoy doing this as well, you could make a career out of it and work for some of your favorite companies. Nickelodeon, Disney, and Cartoon Network are just some of the many companies that hire people to build websites and then make games, animations, or interactive comics to put on these websites. Does that sound like something you could imagine yourself doing in the future? If so, Scratch is the perfect place to start.

Motion

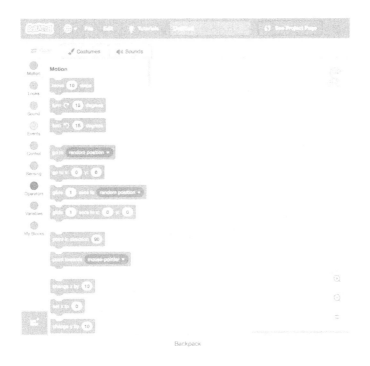

Motion controls the movement of your character or as the design studio refers to them as 'sprites.' The default one is the signature Scratch cat, but there are a lot of other sprites that you can choose from to make engaging stories. However, until you understand the functionality of the studio and all of its features, choosing sprites can wait. So, for now, we'll use the famous Scratch cat to help you learn all of your simple coding needs. Motion control lets your character know whether or not you want it to spin, slide, run, or walk. You can animate the way that they move, how fast they move, and what direction they move in by changing the numbers in the blocks to suit your needs. You can alter these in any way that you like. Change 10 steps to 30, Turn 45 degrees instead of 15, or choose a specific position for the sprite to move towards. After you change the figures to whatever you'd like, it is time to drag and drop these into the white space where they will tell your sprite that it's time to move. For example, let's click 'Move 10 steps' block and drag and drop it into the white space.

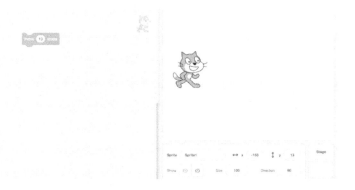

After you've done that, you'll notice now that every time you click on this block that the Scratch cat then moves 10 steps to the right. Pretty cool, huh? This is called running a block. Running blocks is a rewarding way to play out your creation to see how it's coming along, allows you to review it, and make changes to it if you don't like the way it's turning out.

Sound

We can dive a little deeper into this and make our Scratch cat meow! There are many sound options available that can help us out with this. In addition to just adding the sounds, the Scratch studio lets you completely modify it to sound exactly how you want it to. You can make it sound high-pitched like Alvin and the Chipmunks or deep like Darth Vader! You can play around with this feature and make the sounds fade in or out, play it in reverse, make it sound robotic, or make it louder or softer to get it just right. You can even record your own sound and give your characters a customized flair that only you can provide. You can record it right on the Scratch studio by connecting a microphone or speaking directly into your device. If you have some sounds or music that you have saved on your computer, you can use those sound bites for your projects by uploading them.

If you don't have any sound files saved or don't want to record any, there's another option for you! Scratch has a vast sound library that has everything that you could ever need for all of your sound needs. From sound effects to background music to witty catchphrases, everything you could ever want all in one place! There are different categories of sound that can help create the perfect atmosphere for your projects. Maybe your characters take a trip to the zoo with different animal calls belting out as you pass through? Or attend a classical music concert featuring the mellow tones of violins and piano? What about fighting off an army of ninjas in an action-packed fight sequence? Although these ideas are incredibly distinct from one another, they all require one thing to ensure their success. The use of sound.

Sound can help you add to the sense of your project and make it look and feel more real. Have you ever watched a scary movie? Think of the scariest scene you can from your favorite scary movie. If you try watching that same scene, but without sound, it would still be scary but in an unusual way. It feels different from the original, scary, but watered down and not as extreme. Sound can trigger certain emotions or feelings when paired with intense imagery or video. When you choose the right sound, it can completely change the way your project is received by the people viewing it. By choosing accurate sounds to accompany your assignment you can easily influence your audience to feel the same emotions that you had in mind when you were creating it. This is not only constructive for you because your project will appear more complete but good for the person viewing it because they will be able to actively engage and see your personal work for what it is. Usually, if people feel connected to the creator, their work is valued that much more, and they'll want to help them progress and perfect their skills and support their work.

Coding Sound along with Motion

After you're finished choosing and editing the sound clips for your project, it's time to start coding them so that they react with the motions you chose earlier. Drag and drop the sound coding block that best suits your needs into the same white space that you moved the motion block to. You can put it above or below, depending on what coding block you choose. The blocks all have different functions, depending on how you would like your project to run. Like the motion blocks, there are several options that you can choose from that will allow you to create countless combinations of tasks to program certain actions. You can play the sound until your sprite stops moving, play the sound once you begin the action, or stop all sounds after a certain point. You can also set the pitch, volume, or even clear sound effects if you made a mistake. You can do this by dragging and dropping the blocks back to the place you dragged them from, and they'll disappear instantly. You can add these sound blocks to as many motion blocks as you would like to create endless combinations of motions and sounds that will bring your sprites to life.

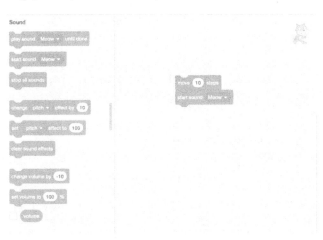

Adding Events

Can you remember what I said earlier about running blocks? Running blocks is a helpful way to determine the needs of a project and decides whether or not the code present processes smoothly. Adding events can help with this and make the activity of running blocks trouble-free and simple so that you can run your lines of code without disruption or without clicking constantly to discover if your code works. These event blocks are very special and can affect the entire section of code depending on how you use them and what you use them for. If you look at the blocks, you'll notice that some of them are shaped differently than the motion and sound blocks. This is because these are meant to be placed on top of the code blocks that you've already added. These being placed at the top means that they are in complete control of the blocks beneath them. You can give specific commands based on what action is in the block. Such as the green flag icon. This flag is located right above the display that contains your sprite and its environment within your program. You can use that block to play the entire function from beginning to end upon clicking the green flag icon. If you have chosen, this block and click the green flag, the entire block order will carry out on the screen.

Running the code

No matter what block you chose, it is encouraged that you do this throughout the duration of your creative process to recognize errors or mistakes as they happen then work towards a solution. Maybe your sound doesn't play as it should, or your animation is choppy and stiff? Recognizing errors like this early on in the coding process can have a big impact on the quality of your project. You can work through solutions throughout the project, which will make sure that you don't encounter any trouble later when you are finalizing the code and producing the project. You have other ways of running your code, such as the "when the ___ key pressed" block. This block allows you to run the code by pressing a key on your keyboard like the space bar or any other alphabetic keys. Some people prefer this as it can be more convenient during the running process because your hands don't leave the keyboard while you're coding. Your decision is subject to what you would rather use as an indicator of when to direct your code. The other blocks offer others choose to run it when your sprite is clicked, a backdrop changes, a specific volume is observed, or a message is received.

Combining all of these blocks through the code after individual sequences of motion and sound blocks can improve the pacing of your animations or games. For example, you can use these blocks before or after small sequences of motion and sound blocks to trigger countless starting points by adding specific details that align with your other blocks. You could specify that you want the loudness of a specific sound bite to be ">10" and then chose the block that allows you to run based on a specific sound volume. As displayed in the picture shown below.

```
when ⚑ clicked
start sound Meow ▼
turn ↻ 15 degrees
turn ↺ 15 degrees
say Hello! for 2 seconds
play sound Meow ▼ until done
move 10 steps
move 10 steps
```

These sequences of blocks are what the majority of your short films, games, and animations will be based on. When you combine all of these sequences into long lines of coding commands, you can then begin building and elaborating on them so that when they perform their unique actions that it complements the other blocks. Your previous blocks must be considered before moving forward to future blocks, as the accuracy of them could compromise the following actions. Think of these sequence combinations as a chain; if one of the links is weak, then the entirety of the chain is in jeopardy. Because of the delicacy of this metaphorical chain, it is of utmost importance that you review how blocks may react to other blocks by running them.

You can use block running as mini-trial and error sessions to determine problems and work towards a solution. This will improve your problem-solving skills, which are valued, especially when you collaborate with other Scratch users, and you eliminate errors throughout the project. Your fellow Scratch users will surely appreciate your quick wit and talents as it will help with the coding process and the quality of your projects. Just play around with the controls to get the hang of them, and you'll pick it up almost immediately.

Look

Now that you've got the basics of the coding to make it run smoothly, it's time to make your project look pretty. Through the Looks tabs, you'll be able to change backdrops, add speech bubbles, and make costume changes. You can set the scene for your sprites and completely customize the environment to add depth to your project and make it visually appealing and stimulating. These aspects of the look blocks are exactly the same as the motion and sound blocks in the respect that you can base the commands of your code later on the decisions you've made in the Look blocks that you've chosen. Such as having a sound play when a specific backdrop is shown or program a speech bubble to appear when your sprite moves. You can create layers as well with this feature meaning that you can overlay sprites and backdrops and push them to the front or back depending on which ones you want to appear in the background or foreground. You can change the size of your sprite or props in the background as well and program them to change size throughout certain points in your project.

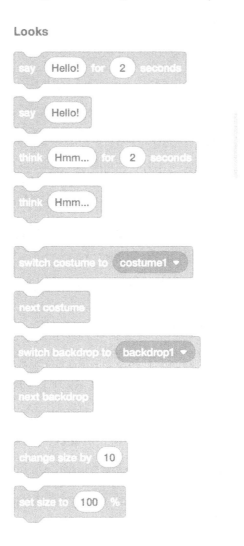

This is helpful because you can isolate the layers and work on them individually without accidentally making unwanted changes to them. Having certain programming tactics assigned to different layers be a big help with staying organized and keeping tracking of your functions. Backgrounds add much-needed depth to your projects because it creates a space for your sprites to interact with others. With the help of the Look block, you can even create your backdrops and upload them onto Scratch! Adding your own artwork can make your project really stand out amongst other studios or projects because no one could ever quite recreate your backdrop the way that you do. People will see your unique backgrounds and know instantly that you made it because of your style. This makes your project one of a kind and gives you more credit as a creator and a Scratch user.

Costume Tab + Look Block

You also can achieve this originality through costumes, which you can customize using the Costume Tab. Costumes meaning the color, brightness, transparency, or boldness of the outline. All of these small components can impact how your project is perceived by your audience and can add much-needed depth to your projects. This closely relates to the contents of the Look blocks because your costumes are saved through this tab and show up as options whenever prompted by a block. You can make a sound play after a costume is changed or modified or even program a speech bubble to appear to transform your sprite.

The costume tab allows you to completely redesign your sprites using custom colors through outlines and fills. You can also change the transparency of the sprite to create some ghoul-y ghost guys or change the skin color to show if someone has become poisoned or hurt! It's completely up to you, depending on the story that you would like to tell. You should use these features to your advantage when creating characters on Scratch. Giving your characters a specific look to convey different emotions or events in relation to different environments and backdrops that can help you to define your project as you would like it to be. These decisions are completely up to you and can have a lasting impact once your project is published for the public to see.

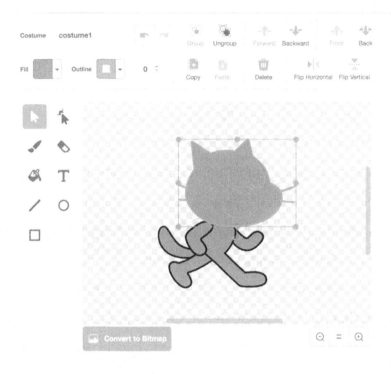

Control

As the name would suggest, the control blocks help you program specific controls to improve your functions as they happen. The control blocks all have certain commands to make controlling the code as simple as it could be. For example, the block labeled 'wait _ second' allows you to program a certain amount of time in between your blocks in the beginning, middle, or end. This can be helpful for the pacing of your project as it makes carrying out commands easy and puts you in complete control of how tasks are performed and in what way. Adding blocks like this lets your instructions be achieved in a timely yet controlled manner. You can repeat commands, put tasks on a continuous loop, or use operators (you'll learn what these are in the next section) as signals of what the next function will be or what it will do. You will do this between sound or motion blocks to maintain a sense of control and to direct them to be in the order that they need to be to make the code run as it should.

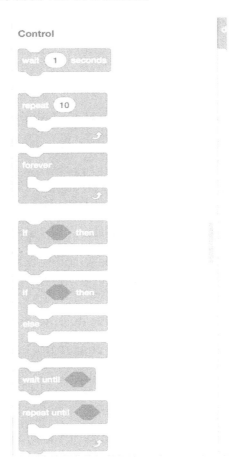

Every line of code has an effect of the ones before or after it, so when creating, you must think about the outcome and how you will get there. Keeping these thoughts while you are creating helps you think of a path towards your goal and makes the process easier if you have an idea of what you want to happen. That way, you plan tasks in advance and put them into action in the order that you think will be the best path to take. These controls can be a useful tool in creating your digital reality. Begin with the end in mind and take steps towards that ending.

Think of what you want to happen and then make it happen. Believe in your talents, and then put the necessary motions in place so that you can achieve it. You've made it this far which means that you have the potential to become a great coder. Just do what you think will be the best thing for you in the situation that you imagine could bring about your desired end results. The lessons you studied before this were preparing for you to be the best coder that you can be and through these blocks and the properties that they hold, you can achieve that. Don't be afraid to ask for help, especially at this stage, because this is probably the most challenging step of the entire process. However, it is not impossible! Have confidence in your abilities and put them to use here. No one is perfect the first time they program or write code, and it is important that you think about that because if an error occurs, don't be discouraged! Run it through again and try again until it works. This may take a while depending on the problem, but remain patient. It will pay off. Use what it takes to solve the puzzle.

Operating

Operating blocks are the instructions that go into the command blocks to help it function and operate in any way that you choose. You can manually edit coordinates or other directions into these blocks. These will give the operating system a more vivid description of exactly what you want to happen. Coordinates are kind of like a map for where you want your sprite to go. If you view the plane through the white space, you can determine the coordinates of your sprite. You can do this by dragging and dropping the sprite, which will make the coordinates will show up in the control panel, which you can change and alter to correlate with positions and movements that you have added. Once you edit the operation, you can put it in within the control blocks to run the code and incite actions to get your work going.

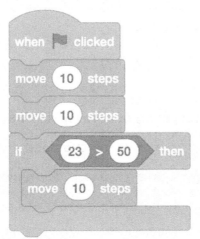

You are welcome to alter anything throughout the process. It is advised that you work on one section at a time. Although you must work with the end in mind, you must also have a productive attitude in respect of working to create rather than working to finish. Take your time with this because it's key to try and figure it out as you go along. If you approach it that way, you can learn, recognize these errors, and work to align your operations with your desired outcome of events. These values are up to you and depending on what you would like to see, and you can alter them gradually in order to carry out the function that you deem appropriate for the completion of your project. Sensing blocks can help you go even further by creating functions that respond to your directly to actions that you perform.

Sensing

Just like the operations block, sensing can help you pinpoint functions by assigning specific actions to whatever function you want to carry out. For example, one of the sensing segments says, "touching mouse pointer?" meaning that if you add this to a control block, you can easily direct your mouse to carry out a function that influences your coding process. Sensing is the keyword here, meaning that if the program senses a specific action such as touching the mouse pointer or touching a specific color that the program will carry out the function as it is written. This is especially helpful when creating computer games or interactive programs. When creating these projects that require input from the user, it is important to keep in mind that although the process is similar to creating animations that projects like this need extra direction. The sensing blocks can help with this and help your games run easily when they are prompted by the user. If you've played games before you know that there are specific controls with a different action assigned to them that allow you to play the game.

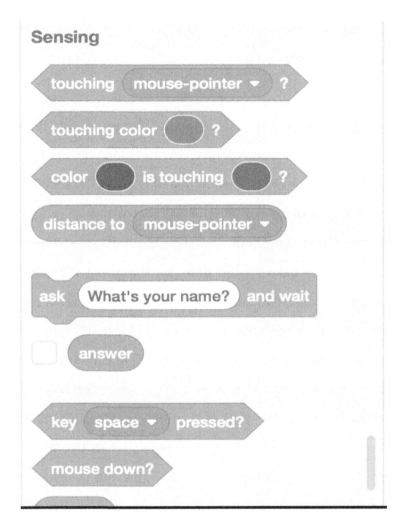

The sensing blocks are the perfect place for you to begin doing this! When you play a game have you've ever been asked to press A to jump or space to run? Sensing has a hand in this and can make the controls come to life so that users can play your game and reach their goals within the game. Depending on what actions you want to go with each keystroke you can use these blocks to program them! Maybe you want the character to run in whatever direction the cursor is pointing or some treasures to appear after they've touched a green vase. Because you have no control of what the user is going to do it's good to account for the things that may happen when they are playing the game. Being aware of actions that may cause trouble when they're playing helps you figure out what you need to put in place to alleviate some of that concern. Of course, if you don't have psychic powers, you may wonder how you will do this? How do I plan for something when I don't know what's going to happen? This may seem impossible for you to pull off, but if you think about all the games that you've played and how they run, it can become second nature for you to program your own controls. Think about what you want the character to do and how the player might make them do this. Should they press a key? Or follow the direction of the mouse? It would be a big thing to ask you to plan every control to account for what might happen and what could happen, but you don't have to. Just think of how you play and make a game, keeping in mind what you do when you play a game. Make a game that you would not only play but could play.

Variables

Have you ever heard of a variable? If you pay attention during math class, you should have heard this word mentioned a couple of times and know exactly what they are and what they do! So, you won't need me to help you! Good luck and goodbye!

I'm just kidding, but if you don't always pay attention to what your teacher says, your desire to learn to code should encourage you to listen more closely. Learning and understanding basic math can help you when coding the basics now or later when you move on to the more difficult assignments when you get older. Although you don't have to be a math whiz to code, learning basic math is a great investment towards your future in the field. Now with that being said, I'll teach you what a variable is and how you can use them in your projects. A variable is something that changes depending on the situation it's in. In math, this is usually shown by x, y, or z. When it comes to coding, a variable is something that changes to suit the needs of your project. These variables can be assigned to your sprites and can change based on what actions that you have programmed. This allows your sprites to come to life in the respect that they will be able to process the code that you put in place but are able to act on their own if a variable is added.

You can set this variable to whatever you want, but be careful because it can have a major effect on the rest of your work. To set a variable first click "Make a variable," then choose the sprite to act under the variable. You'll then edit this variable by choosing a number to go along with it. Now every time your sprite acts under this variable it will change to accommodate the situation that you want it to be a part of. This creates less work for you as it will carry out your request automatically, so you don't have to worry about changing it throughout the project. It's important that you test the success of this variable as soon as you put it in place or it will cause more harm than good. Because variables change automatically, it could cause a change that you don't want to happen to happen constantly. Review your variable by running the code and try to choose a variable that you feel will be the best one to suit your needs and carry out the actions that are expected of it. This requires a lot of planning and thought because adding variable, although extremely beneficial for your project if done incorrectly, can have a negative effect on the rest of your work. Don't be afraid to ask a teacher or friend about this because it's better to be safe than sorry, especially if you've worked hard on something that you want to add variables to.

Blocks

Throughout this chapter, we learned how to use the blocks that Scratch has provided you to create computer games, animations, and interactive stories. These blocks each have unique properties that contribute to the overall quality of the project. Depending on what ones you use and in what way these blocks can make your project the best that it can be. Familiarize yourself with these blocks to develop your skills and understand the basic roles that they offer and how you can use these functions to your own benefit. Become a master of sound mixing, animate your characters in a way that makes Walt

Disney jealous, or make the next best-selling computer game all by learning these through these blocks! Once you've mastered these, this block tab can take you a step further in having complete control and having creative freedom with your projects. You should view these coding blocks funnily enough as the building blocks of your projects, but within these building blocks are even more opportunities for you to alter and control this information to your advantage.

You can create your own blocks here! Add an input – meaning write a direction for your block using numbers or text. Look at the previous blocks that you've used for your project and draw inspiration from there. These directions can be very simple or complex, depending on the nature of your request and how you propose to carry it out. Think of what you want to be done within your project and use the tools here to help you work towards that. Add an input boolean so that you have the option of adding sensing or operating segments to control these aspects directly. That way, the directions that you add into these block templates can react with these segments and bring about amazing and personalized results tailored completely for your own projects and self-satisfaction. Just like how the standard blocks assist in the coding process by directing the codes following it, you can completely rewrite these static actions and add in your own functions. This is helpful because the standard blocks are very limited in their functions, and you don't have many options to change them to suit your needs. You can also add labels to keep them organized and make them easy to locate and access. All of your pending blocks will be located here and will be there for you to change and move as you like.

Chapter 5

Coding Tips and Tricks

Now that you've learned the basics of how to code using Scratch, it's time for you to spread your wings and start diving into the wonderful world of coding! Even though you've read this book, coding requires hands-on involvement in activities to build skill. Meaning that in order to REALLY learn how to code. You have to, well code. This can be scary, especially if this is your first-time coding. But don't worry as long as you remain patient and confident in your abilities, you'll be making those Scratch stories in no time. So, here are some helpful tips and tricks to get the ball rolling for you.

1) **Start small and explore** - Start by creating simple animations using the sprites, and you can build your skills from there. Use different costumes, add more sprites, create backdrops, edit the sound, just add those blocks wherever you can, run them, and see what they can do! Add, remove, or delete, play around with the options that we've talked about and see how they can change your final program. Even the smallest change can have a big impact on the way your project runs. Finding these changes and understanding why they've happened can teach

you how to combine multiple lines of code and know about the end results that they may bring. Explore these combinations and learn from them. You may have dreams of becoming one of the most successful coders in the world. You have to start from scratch and figure out how the system before you can go any further.

2) **Have a plan for your project** – Like anything in life, things go much better when you plan them out. If you start coding straight away, you may find that you've bitten off more than you can chew when you start to get into it. This is because you don't have a goal or a path to get there. You can't work towards anything. You need to have a plan in place to help you decide what you want your project to look like (sprites, backdrops, costumes), how it will operate (what blocks you'll use, what you'll use them for, what information do they need to run), what additional effects you'll use, (sound, music, speech bubbles) and what you want to happen (win game, end of story, animation). When you code planning your project before working on it can save you a lot of time and heartache because you know exactly what you want to do and have an idea of how to do this. That way, you can spend less time trying to figure out what you want and more time actually bringing it to life.

3) **Learn from your mistakes** – Coding in any of its forms is a series of trial and error sessions that will bring you closer to a solution. Trial and error mean that you try something over and over to see if it works. If it doesn't work the first time, you must look for things that could help you improve the project and then try each one to see if they improve the quality of the project. This requires a lot of patience, understanding, and confidence. Patience to see your project for what it could be rather than what it is and working towards that by following your plan but making changes as you go to ensure that it works. Adopt an understanding of the Scratch systems, the controls, and the standards of your project and then use them to your advantage to create, alter, and succeed within your own space at your own pace. It is also important to have confidence in your abilities as a coder and a creator! There's nothing wrong with what you did, how you did it, or you project idea. Some processes just take longer to master and perfect. Don't be discouraged. You've made it this far, and the only direction is forward, work through these projects while believing in your talents and abilities, and it will give you the confidence to continue your work and make your dreams a reality.
4) **Work hard but have fun** – when you're working so hard on something that you care about, it's easy to forget that you're

doing it to have fun. If you get overwhelmed with the amount of work you have to do and find yourself becoming frustrated, angry, or annoyed, remember that you are creating something that you not only want to share with others but share with yourself. You've imagined yourself creating this since you thought of it! Now you're finally creating it! You should be very happy to have this opportunity and have fun with it. It doesn't have to be done fast, so take your time and learn by getting in and doing it. Scratch has tailored its website to be easy and to be fun so that you can gain the skills that you need

5) **Give yourself a break** – when you are coding, it is very easy to get lost in what you are doing. Before you know it, hours might have passed. But always, coding isn't a good thing. You need to take a break from it now and then for many different reasons. The first thing to think about is that if you work yourself too hard, then you aren't going to be doing as good of a job as you can. When you work too long and hard, you get tired, and you start making mistakes when you get tired. Second, you don't want to be too wrapped up in one thing. You probably have other activities that you enjoy, and so you should take time out for them. Being balanced between other fun things to do, engaging in activities with your friends, and keeping up with your schoolwork is all important. Taking a break can also help

you when you are stuck on a hard problem. If you feel like you are banging your head against the wall trying to figure out how to build a script in one of your projects, and nothing seems to work, consider just taking a break. Many times, when we take a break from something that we are having a hard time with, we find it's easy when we come back to it. Taking a break can help you relax and clear your head so that you can work better later.

6) Stay Focused – It can be easy to get distracted. You can start a project and then get an exciting idea for a new project. But you should hold off on the new project until you finish the first one. It can become a problem if you start getting in the habit of not completing tasks that you set out to accomplish. You are going to be better off over the long run if you are able to finish everything that you start. Sticking to your projects in scratch is a great way to learn this valuable habit. Of course, it isn't a law, and there are going to be exceptions to this rule. So, if you find yourself in a situation where you are stuck on getting something to work, and you are not making any progress, it is fine under those circumstances to let it go and try something else.

7) Look for more information online – There are many resources online that can help you learn how to code. Start with videos

on YouTube. Watching someone else do something and having them explain it while they work is a great way to learn. In fact, it is probably the best way to learn that there is. I have to admit that watching videos on YouTube when I want to learn something beats reading a book. You can also check on Udemy, which has many courses. They have some courses on scratch. One course that is a favorite of mine is building 11 games using scratch 3. You might enjoy that and find some others. The courses can help you go through scratch step-by-step, which is one of the best ways to learn how to code. In addition to videos, you can find many websites that have examples that can help you learn how to build your own scripts.

8) Get inspired- A good website to use when learning scratch is the scratch.mit.edu site. There are many existing projects of different types that are posted on the site. You can use these examples to learn and help you get inspired to do your own projects.

9) Get to know your fellow Scratch users- Don't be afraid to reach out for help. It is good to learn scratch on your own, but you should get to know other scratch users. This will help you share ideas and get inspiration from what they are doing. It also helps if you have friends to talk to when you are running into

difficulties, either getting a script to work or getting ideas on how to move a project forward.

Ideas- Keep a notepad so that you can keep track of ideas. Once you start coding, ideas are going to start flowing. You don't want to let them slip by. That doesn't mean that you are going to implement every idea that you come up with, but it will give you a list of fun things to try.

Tutorials- There are many tutorials available online that will help you to learn Scratch and other programming tools. You can find tutorials on the MIT scratch site, and in many other places, for example, there are many easy to follow scratch tutorials that can be found on YouTube.

Coding Cards – Coding cards are a popular tool used with scratch, that help children with step-by-step instructions. Coding cards will help children who are just starting out to learn how to create interactive games, stories, and other projects and activities. There are many free scratch coding cards available, but you can also buy sets of coding cards that can help your child stay engaged after they start picking up more skills and developing further.

Starter Projects – There are many starter projects posted online. Starter projects are simple projects that are already built, which allow the child to play with an existing and already working activity or interactive game. In the process, they are also able to look at the coding scripts that were used to create the activity. This can be a great way for the child to learn and have fun at the same time. It can be helpful for them to see the connections between computer codes and the actions that they see on the screen.

Scratch Desktop Download – the standard way to use Scratch is via an internet connection. However, it is possible to download scratch to your desktop computer and use it offline. This can be useful if you don't want to worry about a Wi-Fi connection, or if you would like some privacy when your child is using scratch. By using it offline, you don't have to worry about anyone seeing what you are doing and so forth. To download the desktop edition that works offline, visit the website link below.

https://scratch.mit.edu/download

Chapter 6

Creating a Plan for Your Project

Many people don't like this concept. The worst thing that you can do when starting a project is to just jump in and start working on it. Instead of doing that, you should think about your project beforehand.

The Importance of having a plan

Let's think about two different types of projects. First, consider a story. You could just open up scratch and then build your story as you go. You could pull up character sprites, and just make up stuff for the characters to say. You could keep doing this until you had a large number of scenes worked out.

The story would complete, but do you think it would be the best possible story?

There might be a better way to come up with a story app for your scratch project. Suppose that instead of just working it out on the fly, you took some time to think about your story first. You could even use a pencil and paper. Start by drawing the main characters. Or you can just write down their names and what they look at.

Think hard about the characters in your story. Who are they and where do they come from? What do they want?

Then build up an overall outline for the story. At this stage, you don't have to fill in all the details. Just outline the main points of the story. You could name each scene you would like to have, and then write out what is going to be said and how things are going to develop. You can also write down some ideas about how each scene is going to transition into the next scene.

Keep in mind that this does not mean you can't change things later on. This is just to help you set up the story and get it to flow in the best way possible. When you plan things out ahead of time, when you get on your computer and start using scratch to actually create the story, this is going to make building your application a lot easier. It will take less time to build it as well, and it's going to come across better to people who watch it.

Again, this does not mean that you can't change the story later on. You can even change it after you have built up all the scenes in scratch. It can be changed at any time. But by planning, we will find that we save a lot of time and energy, and our work usually turns out better than it would if we just rushed ahead with it on the computer.

The more complex the app, the more planning you need

If you are going to design a complicated game, it can help to use the same procedure. If you are building a script that is going to be really complicated, then it is even more important to plan out how you are going to do it first. The worst thing that you could do is jump on the computer and just start trying to build a game or large application without having any idea about how it's going to work and progress.

Let's say that you wanted to make a maze game. A good way to approach this is to draw out all of your mazes on paper before you even open up scratch. You might find that some mazes that look good on paper are too hard to get through when you actually put them up on the computer screen. But one thing for sure is that your building of the game is going to be accomplished in a much shorter time once you get on the computer in scratch than if you had not planned it out ahead of time.

Planning is Best as a Middle Ground

You want to plan out your programs, but don't overdo it. You don't want to write down every last detail. Have you written any papers in school? The way to write a paper is to start by making an outline. You can think of that here. Think of your planning stages for coding as making an outline for your project. Then when you actually start working on it on the computer and building your scripts, you can fill in all the details and potentially make changes.

Use the Planning Stage to Hone Your Ideas

During the planning stage, talk to others that are using scratch, or to your friends. Discuss your ideas with them to see what they think and see if they have some ideas that can make your project even better. It is easier to work things out like this in the planning stage if you are working on a large project. If you dive in to building your project and have a large number of sprites and scripts, having to go into all that detail to make major changes to the scripts can be very time consuming and frustrating. If you are working on a really large project, the project can actually get so complex that it is nearly impossible to change.

Planning with Pseudo Code

When we are working with scratch, we create actual code in our scripts. It can be helpful to plan out your scripts ahead of time by writing what is called pseudocode on a piece of paper. All this means is that you write out the steps that are going to be used in your script. So, we can write something like this:

If a cat touches the green bar then

   Play meow sound

   Increase score by one point

So, in other words, we are basically thinking out and writing down the steps that our program is going to take ahead of time. This is an informal process, and so you don't need to have all the steps laid out exactly.

Think of the time you will save by doing this, though. When you write all the steps out, then opening up scratch and actually building the scripts is going to be so much easier that you are going to be amazed.

Start with the end goal in mind

Start the planning process with two statements. First, write down the starting point of your project. Then, write down the endpoint or goal of the project. So, if someone were to use your application, what is the end result of them doing so? This exercise should be used each time that you decide to start a new project on scratch. Once you have the two endpoints clearly defined, then filling in the intermediate steps to get you from point A to point B is a lot easier.

Draw Scenes on paper

Don't just write out pseudocode when planning out your project. You can actually draw out the scenes the way you want them to look. Are you a lousy artist? Don't worry about that if you are. The point of doing this is not to impress anyone with your artistic ability. You don't even have to show the drawings to anyone else if you don't want to. The point of doing the drawings is for you and to help you get organized and get your project done faster and more efficiently. People who don't plan things out this way can end up wasting a lot of time in front of the computer screen. Wouldn't you rather be efficient and get your work done fast? It will also help you reduce frustration because you can open up your project and start building it quickly, according to the plan that you have already laid out.

Scheduling Your Work

You can also create a calendar and schedule for your project. You can specify what you are going to do on each of the days on the calendar. This will help you work more efficiently, which means that you will get more done in less time.

Chapter 7

What Coding Can Do for You

So far, we have seen a little bit about what coding can do. It can be instructive to start creating programs of your own, but in truth, we are barely getting started. Coding is a skill that can take you far and in many different directions. You can code for fun or learn how to solve many problems, but you can also do many things in the "real world" with coding. For those that find computer programming interesting and fun, the sky is the limit as to what you can do.

At the most basic level, coding is a great way to train your mind to think in more organized and advanced ways. Although math is not directly involved with coding, it is a mathematical way of thinking. Coding can be a way for children to improve their math muscles, even If they are not doing it directly.

Coding also helps you to organize your thoughts and focus. One of the best ways to help mitigate attention deficit disorder is to become a coder. The reason this works is that intense focus is necessary for successful coding. It can help calm the mind, as the child focuses on figuring out a problem and getting it solved.

Coding will help the child develop logically based reasoning skills and learn how to problem solve in general. It can also help deal with frustration and important life skill that all of us should have. In many cases, coding doesn't go the way you hope. The more you develop, the more complicated it gets, and this leads to the inevitable rise in errors. Solving the errors to get things working is something that takes a great deal of patience when you are dealing with large programs. Going through that experience can help children develop the methodical skills that will help them get through virtually any situation in life later on. In addition, they will have to learn patience.

Reasons to Code

There are many different reasons that we can put forward for kids to learn to code. The first is that there is a continued shortage of people who are able to fill STEM jobs. Millions of these jobs are going unfilled, and a shortage means higher wages for those that possess the needed skills.

Learning some coding skills early is something that children can do to help bolster their resume in these competitive times. Even getting into college, or at least the college that you want is something that can be made easier if the child can already demonstrate some practical skills.

Coding can also help children understand the technical world that is all around them. They can understand the internet, smart TVs, and smartphones they can't seem to put down. By understanding how things work, they can also begin to get inspired and think of their own ideas.

Coding Is Used Nearly Everywhere

One of the best things about coding is that the more widespread computer use becomes, the more areas of life that are touched by coding. This means that no matter what you are interested in, coding can play a role. For example, if you like music, there are many applications of coding in the music industry. Or, if you like airplanes, coding is used extensively to help the plane fly and get home safely. Coding is even used in sports, where coaches are using it to help their teams perform better. It seems like no matter what, coding is being used in any area of life that you find interesting and fun. When you can do computer programming that is applied to something that you find interesting, you are going to find that you enjoy coding and will find work fun.

Coding Can Make You Smarter and Improve Your Self-Confidence

You have probably seen people that go to the gym and exercise a lot. People that lift weights gain a lot of muscle. Other people that run or ride bikes get stronger and healthier. It turns out that the brain works in the same way. Your brain is just like a muscle. If you sit around and don't exercise at all, your muscles will shrink from a lack of use, and the body becomes weak. Older people who never exercise get out of breath just walking around.

The same thing happens to your brain. If you don't use it, then it won't develop and become strong. But if you work your brain by challenging it, the brain becomes stronger, literally making you smarter. The more you work your brain, the smarter you are going to get.

You may notice that if you practice doing math problems, they get easier for you. Or the more you study for an exam, the easier it is to remember what you need to know. And you become more confident about the right answers.

Coding is one of the best ways to challenge your brain and help you become smarter. Although people who haven't gotten any experience doing computer coding find it scary, when you take it slow and learn it step-by-step, you find out how natural it really is. Computer coding is nothing more than doing what comes naturally to humans. Let me explain.

Ever since there have been humans, we have relied on problem-solving to help us survive. Compared to other animals, humans are slow and weak. We have trouble surviving outdoors unless the weather is in a very narrow range of temperatures because we don't have any fur. It is hard for us to catch animals to eat because we are a lot slower than most animals. We can't run very fast, and we run out of energy very quickly compared to them.

What made the difference? Our brains made the difference. In other words, we used our ability to think. People used their minds to think of better ways to do things. This led them to figure out that they could survive cold nights by using animal skins to make clothing. Then they devised strategies to hunt, allowing them to use thinking for hunting the animals they needed to eat rather than trying to track them down using sheer speed and strength. They also invented many tools, to help them hunt using spears and arrows, and to cut things so they could use what they found in the environment, including preparing food to eat. Long ago, someone figured out how to use fire as another way of staying warm at night, and also to keep dangerous animals away.

This has been going on throughout history. People have continued to find out new and better ways of doing things, and this helped create civilization. This process is still going on today.

It turns out that computers are a natural fit for the human mind, even though at first people don't feel this way about them. Computers are really just an extension of the human mind, and coding is just step-by-step problem-solving. So, it's not any different than any of the activities people have always engaged in.

When you get to work building a computer program, you are exercising the muscles of your brain, engaging in problem-solving activities. The more you do it, the better you are going to get at problem-solving. Coding teaches you to think carefully and to consider everything that can impact the problem at hand. It will also teach you how to look at how things will change, as each step in a computer program is executed. Not everyone has the same abilities, so some people are going to be better computer programmers than others. But that isn't what's important. The thing to remember is that everyone is going to be smarter than they were before they tried coding if they devote some time to learning this valuable skill.

The more you learn, the better your programming and problem-solving skills become. You can start off building simple programs, and then each time you tackle a new problem. You can build a more complex program.

You Don't Need to Be A Programmer to Benefit

A large part of living in today's world is understanding how things work. If you have some background in coding, even if you are not a computer programmer by trade, having that background will help you understand how the technology around you works. No matter what you do, this will help you do it better. You will understand how to use different tools in your environment, and have a better feeling for how they work, and what can go wrong. Computers touch nearly every aspect of our lives today, and so this means you are not going to have a hard time finding ways that coding can help you understand things.

Almost everything has a computer program in it or associated with it that helps it work. As time goes on, more things are going to have computer programming in them. All around us, there are opportunities for people who know how to code to modify things and make them better. People are always looking at software tools and thinking about ways they could be improved. Even if you are not able to actually program something, it is a good exercise to look at everything and think about how you could improve it. Are there ways something could be easier to do? Could it be done faster or more efficiently? Try thinking about these things as you go throughout your day. For example, you can think about this when you are playing games on your phone or tablet. When playing a game, it's not that hard to think of ways that the game could be better.

You can also do this when interacting with everyday computer applications that you have in your own life. When you open up Netflix to find something to watch on TV, have you ever thought about how Netflix could work better to make it easier for you? Maybe you can think of ways that Netflix could make it easier to find your favorite program, or to find new shows, for example.

Coding as a Career

One of the best things about coding is that there are always jobs available. In fact, it's projected that the number of jobs around for people that know how to code is going to keep increasing. These kinds of jobs pay lots of money as well.

As we said earlier, coding touches every aspect of life. If you enjoy coding, you will probably enjoy doing coding for the sake of coding – and that means you can have fun developing computer programs for any reason. However, the real benefit of coding is that you can specialize in areas that you are interested in. If you like to help people and you're interested in health, you can work in the medical field, developing software programs for doctors and nurses to use while diagnosing and treating patients.

Children will be excited to learn that they can have a career in developing video games. Parents might find themselves put off a bit by this, but don't be. The video game industry is very large, and there are many jobs for coders in this area. By 2019, the video gaming industry had grown to $120 billion in value. According to Microsoft, two billion people are playing video games, and as the use of technology continues to grow, the number of video game players grows too. This means that for many years to come, this is going to be a rapidly growing industry, with lots of jobs. Even better, these jobs can pay very well. This is a great opportunity for kids; they can actually get a job doing something they already love. And they will get paid well at the same time.

As children get older, many will get different interests. Coding applications span nearly everything, and one area where computers are used extensively is in national security. There are many good-paying jobs available for young people who have mastered coding in the defense and national security areas. And within these fields, the number of opportunities is nearly endless and quite varied. For example, many coders work with space vehicles and satellites. A space vehicle doesn't just fly around, it needs computer programmers to help guide it, and somebody has to write the code that will help a satellite operate properly. Coders also help satellites transmit information back to earth, and programs written by other coders help to process data and information sent back to earth by satellites and other space vehicles. You can code for weather satellites, the space station, or robots that explore Mars.

One of the biggest areas for coders when it comes to careers is building simulations. A simulation is a computer code that simulates something in real life so that people can study different problems and their solutions. We all know about climate change; a lot of the information about climate change comes from models that coders build in order to study how different things impact that climate. You can use simulations for almost anything, which makes this an interesting field to get into. You can simulate auto traffic, earthquakes and their effects, the weather like tornadoes and hurricanes, airplane flights, and even people's shopping behavior. Virtually anything that happens can be simulated on a computer, and people that are interested in doing studies in order to learn things will hire coders to help them build simulations. This is another area where you can bring together your interest in coding with interest in something else. Imagine how fun that would be!

The arrival of smartphones has also expanded the world for coders and opened up many new career opportunities. Once again, this is something that has a wide range of applications. Many coders build applications that help people take better pictures for their Facebook and Instagram pages. Others build applications for business, while still more coders are involved in creating games that are played on mobile phones. It's estimated that Apple's iPhone has created 1.5 million jobs in the United States for people that work around the iPhone and not directly for Apple. This includes not only coders but designers, apps have to look nice to attract people to use them. In many cases, coders are also doing a lot of app design work too. These are also well-paying jobs that open up many opportunities for coders to earn a living.

Machine Learning and Data Science

Over the past decade, an entirely new area has opened up that provides even more opportunities for those who start learning to code while they are young. These are the areas of machine learning and data science. Machine learning is a branch of a field called artificial intelligence. For kids who like robots and androids that they see in science fiction movies, this provides an exciting opportunity.

Although you probably think that people are out of the picture when you hear the words "artificial intelligence," nothing could be further from the truth. It is true that it is a more advanced and sophisticated branch of computer work, but many people are working in research building computers that have artificial intelligence. With each passing year, the role of artificial intelligence continues to grow.

Knowing how to code is the first step towards a career in this area. Those who work in this area don't have any problems finding a job, and the jobs are well-paying. And even though the goal of building such computers is to create computers that don't need to be programmed in the conventional sense, it turns out that humans play a direct role in their development. In fact, a new field of study called data science has arisen out of the development of machine learning. This development was also driven in part by the collection of large amounts of data by companies and government agencies. For this reason, people that work in this area are called "data scientists."

Data scientists actually do some coding, but the computer mostly learns on its own. So, for the most part, a data scientist works with computer systems on a higher level, but you are not going to be able to be a data scientist without learning how to code in the first place.

Training to Code

There are many different paths that you can take to become a coder and get a good-paying job. The most straightforward way to do this is to earn a degree in computer science. Keep in mind, however, that computer science involves a lot more than just coding. Computer science does involve a lot of coding, but it is a branch of mathematics and engineering. So, it is a sophisticated field that involves training in the theoretical as well as practical aspects of computer programming. Getting a degree in computer science can be a stepping stone to a career in coding, or doing something more sophisticated like working in artificial intelligence.

At this level, there is a division between hardware and software. Another field that is related to coding is called computer engineering. This is a multidisciplinary field that involves engineering, coding, and a bit of computer science. Computer engineers must master many of the aspects of electrical engineering, and then they focus on computer hardware. Computer engineers learn how to design computer hardware, including the chips that make computers run. They also learn a great deal about coding and do plenty of coding, as well. This can be done at a high level, and also at low levels where they write code to instruct the computer chips directly, in a language that they understand. This can be quite challenging to master, but computer engineers are highly sought after, and so there are always good-paying jobs available in this field.

Many business schools also offer specialized training in computer coding that is business-oriented. This is an easier way to get into the field that can still make you very valuable to companies and help you land a high paying job. As a part of this training, you will learn how to code using computer languages that are specialized for business applications, and you will learn to work with many tools used by large businesses such as SQL databases.

You can also learn to code without getting one of these degrees in college. Many trade schools and community colleges are teaching coding from a practical standpoint. For many applications, including some that we have discussed, like building video games, it can be important to be a good programmer and have good coding skills, but you don't need to know computer science or engineering. Even so, basic coders are still in high demand and can get good-paying jobs. They can also work in a wide variety of fields.

Building Your Skills Over Time

If you think that computer coding is something that you enjoy doing and would like to do for a career, the best way to prepare yourself is to keep learning. Starting early can give children a leg up. Think about this with any skill. Those who begin playing piano early or playing soccer while young are going to have a big advantage as compared to those who wait until they are older in order to take up such activities. While it can be possible for a late starter to get the skills they need, that means you are in for an uphill struggle.

The same is true for coding. Children can begin learning to code at a young age and start developing the thought processes needed for coding. They might start off doing simple tasks, like programming a computer clock, a calendar, or learning how to build a simple game. But as time goes on, they can learn more coding skills and build more complex applications and learn how to build more sophisticated games. At each step along the way, children can slowly learn how to do more difficult computing tasks.

Coding provides many benefits to children, but one of the most important of these is coding translates into general intellectual skill. Coding requires you to break down problems into simpler parts. It helps you to try and see different angles that come with a problem. It also helps you to see other perspectives, since there are many different ways to code a computer program to accomplish a different task. As problems get more complicated, they require many people to work on them. So, although the stereotype is of people working alone, coding is often done in teams. This can help children learn how to work with others and to hear other perspectives.

Coding also helps keep your memory sharp, and even if math isn't directly used in a particular program, coding helps you to think mathematically. As a result, people who develop coding skills tend to find that learning math is easier for them.

So, although not all children who learn to code are going to become professional computer programmers when they grow up, many will find that the enhanced skill set they have developed by learning some coding has helped them in many different areas.

Learning to Build a Toolbox

Computer coding is often built up from individual blocks of code that each solve a specific task. As children begin to learn how to code to solve more complicated tasks, they will find that a part of learning how to code is building codes that can be reused and applied in different situations. This is not only an important part of coding itself, but it's also an important part of becoming a better problem solver in life generally. Think about the times when a new problem might crop up, and you remember something you learned in a different situation that can help you now.

Computer coding can work like that too. Coders build up blocks of code in independent units that go by different names. They can be called modules or libraries. A library might be a set of computer programs that are used over and over again in many different situations. There is no point in reinventing the wheel; once someone has learned how to solve a particular problem, and they have put the solution into a computer code, that solution can be used in any context where that problem may arise.

Children can also learn about the "black box" concept in this context. This idea is based on the concept of having a closed system that solves a given problem, and all you have to do is pass the inputs to the black box, and then it gives you the outputs you need. A black box can be a part of a "plug and play" type system. That is, anytime you need the function that the black box provides, you can plug it into the code that you are building for a new task.

This approach to coding helps save time and effort. In many cases, coding will involve not coming up with a completely original solution to a problem, but rather assembling many previous solutions to other problems that are subsets of the new problem that you are working on. This approach is very common, and when you begin writing programs at the "real world" level, there is never a time when it's not used to some degree or another.

Chapter 8

Activities and Games

In this chapter, we are going to go through some activities that can be followed to learn more about scratch 3. We will discuss how to proceed in order to create some simple games.

Flappy Bird

Flappy Bird is a simple game that caught the world by storm a few years back. It relied on simple game mechanics but was one of the most addictive games ever. In this section, we will show how to create Flappy Bird using Scratch 3.

The first step is to create a new project. The idea behind the flappy bird is that the bird is flying against a blue sky, and you have to tap the bird to help him fly and avoid obstacles. So, the first thing we want to do is change the background. Find a nice blue-sky image.

- Click Choose Backdrop.
- Select "Blue Sky."
- Set size to 100 and direction to 90.

Next, we need to pick our main character for the game.

- Delete any sprites already in the game.

- Click on Choose a sprite.
- Select a bird or parrot.
- Keep direction the same.
- Set size to 20. You can experiment with sizes of 18 to 25 to see what you like best.

The last step is actually pretty important. One of the mistakes that game designers make is creating a character in their game that is too large. You want the character large enough so the character can be seen, but if the character is too large, it can make the game too difficult to play. A larger character will be colliding with obstacles all the time, and this makes the game too hard to be fun.

To have the game work, we have to add gravity to the scene. We can do this by programming the bird to be affected by gravity. Set when clicked to forever and set the value to -3. This will ensure that if nothing else happens, the bird will be pulled to the ground with a gravitational force of -3.

In the real Flappy Bird game, when you tap the screen, the bird gets a boost in the air, so he doesn't fall down. Using our coordinates, x is across the screen, and y is up and down, so y is the coordinate that is impacted by gravity. On your computer, you can use the press of the space bar to accomplish this task with scratch. This can be done by adding a when -> spacebar pressed -> glide to a position. Set x to x position, and then set y to y + 35. When you play the game, see how this works out. If it doesn't work out exactly the way you want it to, then you can change the value, say to y + 40.

You also want your bird to animate. Sprites come with animations for birds to flap their wings. We need to tell the computer to run the animation that comes with the sprite. This is done using when clicked ->forever->next costume. Also, use the wait command, which will tell the computer how fast to run the animation. Use wait 0.5s.

Be sure to tell scratch to keep the blue-sky background in the game at all times. This can be done by setting when clicked -> switch backdrop to Blue Sky.

Now let's create the obstacles used for the bird. In the original Flappy Bird game, the obstacles were green pipes. When the bird either falls to the ground or collides with a pipe, the bird will die, and it will be game over.

For the purposes of this exercise, you can just draw pipes to include in your game. Select the paint button, and draw two green rectangles with a space in the center.

We also need to keep track of the score in the game. Open the Variable section, and click Make a Variable. Select for all sprites, and name it Score. Click the OK button to save it, and then when you see it in the list of variables, click the checkmark to make it visible.

If the bird collides with the ground or a pipe, then we want the game to end. The game should display a game over screen to let the player know what happened. You can design your own backdrop to use and add the words "Game Over" to the screen however you like. But the words should be readable to the player.

Now let's determine when the bird will die and end the game if the bird collides with the ground. This can be done using an if...then statement. We want to use the if statement to test and determine whether the bird has hit the ground. There are two ways to do it. You can check the y-coordinate of the bottom of the blue-sky image, and then have the game change the backdrop to the Game Over screen, indicating that the bird has crashed with the ground. If the blue-sky image has a ground included with it, if the bird collides with the ground, then you can call it game over. The way to detect this is to check to see if the bird has touched the color of the ground. Use the color picker to get the color of the ground, and then use if...touching color..then.

If this condition is met, then we want to display the game over the backdrop. We also need to tell the computer to stop running the game when this happens, so add stop-> All.

When you have added your pipes sprite to the game, we need to add a rule so that if the bird collides with the pipe, the game will end. First, we need to tell the pipe to move to the left, and this is done by decreasing the x coordinate by two. So, under when clicked for the pipe, add set x to 360 and then add a one-second delay by adding wait 1 second.

Now we need to determine where the pipe is, and recycle is so that the bird will encounter pipes over and over again as it flies. We can do this by resetting the x position of the pipe when it has moved to the left off the screen. We also want to increment the score if the pipe passes, but the bird did not collide with it. This can be done by using:

If x position < -170 then

   Set x to 320

   Change score by 1

On the other hand, if the bird collides with the pipe, then we need to end the game. This can be done as follows:

If touching bird then

   Switch backdrop to Game Over

   Stop All

The game would be quite boring with just one pipe to cross, even though it will appear over and over. So, duplicate the pipe object, so we have another pipe in the game. You can start with it having the same properties, but now change the wait time to 5 seconds. Doing this will ensure that the second pipe trails behind the first pipe. To make it interesting, edit the pipe's costume. Change the location of the gap. The changing location of the gap is essential so that it adds some challenge to the player when they are trying to control the bird.

How to Make a Quiz Game

Now let's try a different type of game. This time we are going to consider making a quiz. On the mobile app stores, quiz games are very popular. For a time, Trivia Crack was one of the most downloaded games on the app store.

To make a quiz game, you will have to know how to ask the user questions, and then check to see if their answer to the question is correct. If they give the right answer, then you can award them a point.

Questions can be added to a game using the sensing tab. Scratch 3 has a preset item we can use called "ask and wait." You can use this to ask your questions, and then use if-then statements to check and see if the user has input the correct answer.

The following setup shows how you can add a question to your game. This can be done using the if..then..else construct after the ask and wait. We can ask about the color of scratch cat's fur, for example. It will look like this:

```
ask What colour is Scratch Cat's fur? and wait
if  answer = orange  then
    say Good job! for 2 secs
else
    say That's incorrect! for 2 secs
```

The structure of the quiz can vary depending on your taste. For example, we can add pictures to the quiz along with a nice backdrop to make it look better. You can even have the picture as a part of the quiz. Many famous games that are very popular quiz games ask players questions about pictures. One interesting game to create would be to show pictures about different locations, and then ask the player what location is shown in the picture. For example, you could use a picture of the Eiffel Tower and ask the user what country it is, and the correct answer would be France.

Rather than manually adding a bunch of questions like this, you can create a list-based program. A list will enable you to store a lot of information in an accessible format. For example, we can make a list of 10 questions. Then we can make a list of the answers to the questions. This time we need a variable to get the question and the corresponding answer. This is because the elements of the list are going to be indexed, so you need a number to pick them out. For example, I could have a list of states:

States = {Arizona, California, Delaware, Florida, Georgia, Maine, Rhode Island, Texas}

If the elements of the list were numbered 1 to 8, we could use a number to pick out elements in the list.

States[2] = California

States[6] = Maine

The *length of* function which is built into Scratch will tell us how many items are in a list. Of course, if we had a quiz game that simply went in order through the list, and it played the same every time, that would be boring. To get around that, we can use the *pick random* function. This will generate a random number. So, for our example with the states list, we would want a random number between 1 and the length of States.

We can also play sounds. Adding sounds to a game helps make it more fun for the user and keep them engaged. You can use the correct and incorrect sounds and play the appropriate sound, depending on how the player answered.

The following example from the Scratch Wiki shows how to set this up. The example assumes that we have two lists, questions, and answers. It also uses a variable called item# to randomly pick a question from the list to ask the user. If the user gives the wrong answer, in addition to playing the incorrect sound, the game will also tell the user what the right answer was. If the purpose of the game is for education, then helping people learn by showing them the correct answer will help them do better next time.

The complete code looks like this:

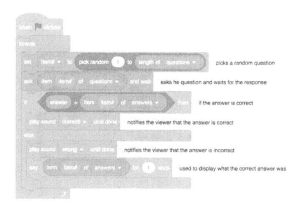

Quiz setup, from scratch-wiki.

Eating Burgies

This is a game posted at scratch.mit.edu. This is a good project to learn from because it brings together many different elements. The game includes background music, an animated character, and a sound when he eats a burger. The burgers also move to the character's mouth when he opens it, and the game includes some animated text.

Him Busy eating Burgits

The animation is created by looping through multiple costumes. Here is costume 1:

At costume 10, we see that a burger has moved into the character's mouth. These events are simply drawn in order, showing the character opening his mouth for a burger, and then the burgers move into his mouth.

The code that executes the animation just cycles through the costumes in order:

When the character eats a burger, there is a gulping sound. The gulping sounds are set up like this:

Sound

- play sound gulp3 ▾ until done
- start sound gulp3 ▾
- stop all sounds
- change pitch ▾ effect by 10
- set pitch ▾ effect to 100
- clear sound effects
- change volume by -10
- set volume to 100 %

Platformer Game

Ever since video games were first created, platformers have been really popular. They are fun because they can be fast-paced and challenging. Let's take a look at some of the aspects of a platformer game using an example called Glitch from the MIT website.

Here we see the main character, a green-colored square. When the game starts, he is resting on the ground below. The game allows control using the keys on your keyboard. For example, we can make the character jump by pressing the w key. So how do we accomplish this in code? The first thing you want to do is check to see if the w key is pressed, using an if key pressed statement. You can choose what direction you want the character to move using x speed or y speed. So, if you want the character to jump up off the ground, we are going to change the y speed of the character. This can be done in the following way:

In a platformer game, you want the character to move to the right also. You can have the character respond to the arrow keys to move either left or right. The following code will help us do this, allowing the character to jump to the right if both w or the arrow key are pressed:

Something that you have to account for in a platformer game is when the player reaches the next level. You will have to build out multiple levels if you make a platformer game, and the distance that the character travels, as measured by checking the value of the x-coordinate, can be used to test for reaching the next level of the game. You can reposition the character at the starting position for the next level.

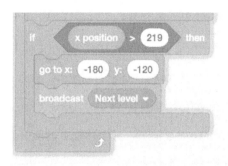

In this game, it has obstacles called viruses. If you touch a virus, it fades the character for a second and makes them go backward. To fade the character, you can use ghosting.

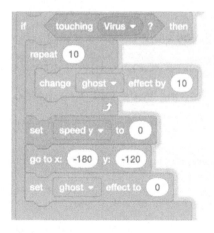

Using the example from the flappy bird game, we could, of course, have the character die and go to a game over screen.

To change levels in the game, as we saw above, you use a broadcast. A broadcast receiver listens for the broadcast to know that the new level condition has been reached.

`broadcast do-this-thing` sends a signal to all parts of the project

`when I receive do-this-thing` a receiver script which will respond to the broadcast

Activity: Change Level when touching a color and Change character

It can make the game more fun if you change backdrops when there is a level change. This helps the player understand that they are on a new level, and it makes it more interesting because things are different. Rather than using distance, this time, let's imagine that we pick a color that will be included in the game scene, and when the character touches the color, this will cause the game to progress to the next level. The first step in this process is pretty straightforward. You want to use

If touching color then

   Do your actions here

To change the way the character looks, you can use switch costumes. We can also change the backdrop used to make the new level look different. Finally, you can use goto x to move the character to a new position on the screen. Typically, if you are moving to a new level, you want to move the character back to the left side of the screen.

Setting up a Story

Scratch can be used to create all kinds of games. So far, we have seen some ways to create motion games like platformers. Another way to create a game is by using a story. In a story, you can have different scenes and interactive characters. You can have your characters move around and say things. So, this can require you to create animation frames for a costume, and a backdrop for your scene. As you move to a different scene, you will change the backdrop and characters.

The first thing to do is set a backdrop for the first scene. This is done in the usual way. Then decide what characters you want to add to your scene. Then decide what they are going to do and say. Getting from one scene to the next is something that you will have to consider when making your story. Go to the state in the lower-left corner of your screen to pick your backdrops to use in the animated story.

Once you have chosen a backdrop, pick the sprites to use in the story. You can draw them or use existing sprites. When you create a new project, by default scratch, the cat will be on the scene. You can delete him and replace him with the characters (sprites) that you want to use.

Once you have the scene setup, you can use scripts to have the sprites engage in a dialogue. This will help to move the story along and entertain your users.

To determine what is done by each of the characters, click on the character you want and then build a script for that character.

Let's suppose you want one of the characters to say hello to another character. You can drag in a when clicked even block to the scene. Then you can go to looks and choose say hello for a given number of seconds. After the character has said hello, you might want to have the other character in the scene say something in response. To make this happen, you have to let the other character know it's time to speak. In order to do this, broadcast a message.

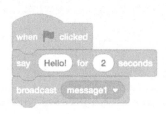

Now let's add an elephant to our scene and have him respond when the cat says hello.

To make the elephant respond when the cat says hello, we want to have the elephant respond to the broadcast message. This script for the elephant will look like this.

So, we'll have the elephant say, "What are you doing cat?" after the cat says hello.

You can then have the elephant broadcast a message back to the cat, to prompt the cat to respond. So, we can change our script as follows:

Now when the cat receives message 2, the cat can respond, saying, "Looking for a mouse!":

```
when [flag] clicked
say  Hello!  for  10  seconds
broadcast  message1

when I receive  message 2
say  Looking for a mouse!  for  2  seconds
```

Using this technique, you can have your characters engage in conversation for as long as you like. You can also have them move around the scene as the conversation progresses, and have the scene change when a character touches a specific color in the scene, for example. When that happens, you can change the backdrop, and reposition the characters, or introduce new characters to your story. By having the story progress through multiple scenes, you can build up a complete story that goes from beginning to the middle, to end.

Animate Your Name

This is a good project because it is relatively simple. We will learn how to write the letters of our name and then have them animate. The letters can dance around, spin, or whatever you can think of. Letters can be found in the costume tab.

First, think about changing the size of a letter. After you have added a letter to the scene, click on the letter so you can build a script for it.

Under looks, you can select a change size block, and specify the scale. To have the letter grow, enter a positive number. The default setting is change size by 5. To have the letter grow even larger, you could say change size by 8, or any other larger number. To shrink the letter, you put a negative sign. So, change the size by -5 will actually shrink the letter.

To have the letter expand and then return to its original size, you first do:

Change size by 5

Change size by -5

When you execute this script, you will find that the letter changes the size so rapidly you might barely notice it, if at all. To avoid this problem, go to events and put a wait block in between, and set it to some delay, like 0.5 seconds. So now our script will follow these instructions:

Change size by 5

Wait for 0.5

Change size by -5

To get your letter to rotate, you can use motion blocks to turn left or turn right. You can change the values used to get the kind of effect that you want. To have the letter animate as long as the script is running, add a forever block around your script. To ensure that the letter starts out in a normal upright position, use a point in direction 90 motion block at the beginning of your script. That way, when the script starts running, it will have the letter start off in the normal upright position.

Navigating a Maze

Building a maze is pretty easy in scratch. All you have to do is add obstacles to your scene that your character has to get around in order to find a path through the maze. You also have to be able to move the character around the screen in all four directions. That is up, down, left, and right.

In order to have the character move, we can specify which direction the character is going to move, and how many steps the character will move in response to a keypress. This means we need to know how many degrees correspond to which direction we want the character to go. But let's not get ahead of ourselves. How do you set it up so that the character starts at the right position at the beginning of the maze? You do this with the green flag event. Then use a motion block to move the character to the right spot.

Here is the maze. The blue blocks are the barriers that the character can't cross. The green block in the lower right corner is the end goal of this level of the maze. If the character sprite touches the green block, then you can create a new scene, for example.

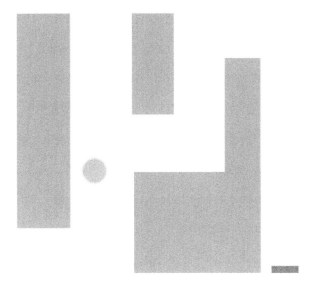

The angles used for directional movement are 0 for up, 90 for to the right, 180 to move down, and -90 to move to the left. These can be set up to work with the up, right, down, and left arrows, respectively. To move the character, we first point the sprite in the appropriate direction, depending on the arrow key that was pressed. Then we have the character move 10 steps.

So, how do we handle the case where the ball runs into a barrier? We can use a simple touch color rule to implement this and have the character do something in response to touching the color of the barrier. In short, by making it take steps backward, that is having a motion block that says move -10 steps, we can have the effect of having the character bounce back when it collides with the blue block.

This should be in force as long as the game is active, so we can use a forever block to implement this. We start the script with a when... clicked block with the green flag, so that this rule is enforced as soon as the player begins the game.

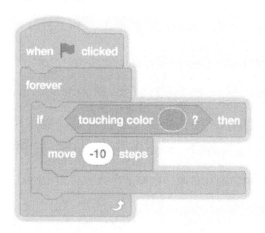

Playing Background Music

Many games have background music. Some games will change the background music when the main character dies, or when moving to a different scene. Simply playing background music for your game is pretty easy. To have sound play from the beginning of the game, use the when green flag clicked block from events in your script.

Then add a play sound block. It will play until the sound file is completed:

If your sound isn't as long as it takes to play the level of your game, you might want to have the sound continually repeat. This is easily done by putting a forever block around the play sound block:

Or, you could have the sound repeat a given number of times. If we want the meow sound to repeat 5 times, we would go to events and use repeat block instead of forever.

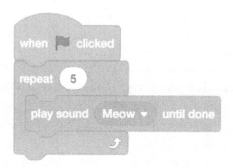

Now suppose we wanted a sound to keep playing until some action was taken. In many games, they will let the player turn off the sound if they like that better. We can use a repeat...until block to do this. For example, we could have the meow sound keep playing unless the user presses the space bar. This can be done by using repeat until...keyspace pressed. It will look like this:

Knowing the different ways that you can use sounds in your programs is important. Using sounds can help to make your games and stories more interesting and entertaining. Sounds can be used to enhance the game, reveal clues, and more.

Exit the Stage

Now let's return to our story. Now say we want the character to exit the stage when they receive a message. You can have the conversation go on as long as you like. Then when the character receives a message, you can change the costume and have the character exit the stage to the right.

We will have the cat say what he is going to say, then have him meow one time, before the costume changes, and the cat slips off the stage. This can be done with the following script:

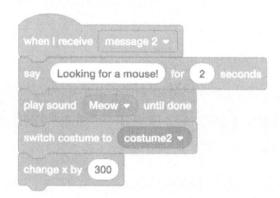

Chapter 9

25 guided activities

- Gameshow
- Animate your own name (done)
- Doodle Jump (done)
- A game like Angry Birds (almost done)
- Mini Movie (needs to run)
- Dress up Game (add music)
- Space Avengers (almost done)
- Digging to the center of the Earth
- Dino Party
- Animated Story
- Create your own character
- Animated Tutorial
- Puzzle Game
- Platformer Game
- Tank Battle Game
- Maze
- Make a calendar
- Quiz Game Flags

- Halloween Story
- Match 3 Game
- Hidden Object Game
- Hair Style Game
- Scrolling Scenes
- Make a clock
- Shooting Game

Chapter 10

Programming Languages and Tools to Learn

In this chapter, we are going to discuss some of the many computer languages and programming tools that are available to use. At this point, this information is for setting up the long-term direction of children who are learning to code. These are tools that are used in real-world applications, but in many cases, there is no reason why children can't start learning to use these tools early. The same approach to programming can be used, starting off doing basic tasks and building up as time goes on, and children gain more experience. In the first sections, we will talk about the different computer languages that are used to give some familiarity with what's out there.

High-Level vs. Low-Level Languages

Computer languages come in many forms. The first thing that distinguishes computer languages is the level at which the language operates. At the hardware level, a computer is basically an organized set of circuits, and the language is really whether or not an electrical current flow or not. This is a yes or no question, and so at the lowest level, computer languages are represented by a set of 1's and 0's. This is called the binary language. In the early days of coding, programmers had to figure out all the 1's and 0's that were necessary in order to have the computer perform a given task. Since thinking in these terms is very difficult, programming was really a specialized task back then. The programmer had to punch holes in a paper card, which was called a punch card. The presence or absence of a hole in the card corresponded to 1's and 0's, and the computer would use light to read in the information, so if light passed through or didn't pass through, it would know there was a hole there or not.

As time went on, experts in the field noticed that this procedure made computer programming difficult and time-consuming. They figured that computer programming was a lot more difficult than it needed to be. So, they developed the concept of a higher-level language. A higher-level language is one that allows the programmer to write a series of statements in English. Of course, this is not English that you would use when speaking to someone; it's kind of rigid for that. But it is simple enough so that people can understand the instructions in a language that they can understand. Although the thought processes used in programming are still hard to master because it involves giving the computer a series of steps it can use to solve a problem, it was much easier than using punch cards and trying to think in terms of "binary." This helped to open up coding to more people since it was easier to deal with.

At first, there were only a few languages, but over time more languages were invented. Some were invented for the express purpose of making coding easier to do. Others were invented to accomplish specific tasks or to be used in certain situations.

Engineers still needed to program computers at a lower level, so a special type of language was invented called assembly language. This breaks down the tasks a computer has to perform into single steps. For example, the programmer can tell the computer to move some data to a specific location in memory. Even though this type of programming gives computers step by step instructions, it is not in the binary format that programmers originally used. It's still pretty hard to learn, but those who are up to the challenge can become computer engineers.

The First Computer Languages

One of the first high-level languages that were developed is called Fortran. The purpose of this language was (and still is) to build programs for scientific purposes. Although it was first developed in the late 1950s, Fortran is still used today in many places. Fortran is really good at doing numerical calculations, and it is pretty easy to learn.

After Fortran was developed, there were some other languages that were created to extend what high-level languages can do and to make coding easier. The first of these is a language called c. Like Fortran, c was developed largely for scientific and engineering purposes, but it is more sophisticated than Fortran. Since c can do a lot more, it quickly became more popular than Fortran.

Basic is another computer language that was developed at about the same time. The name is appropriate since the goal of creating Basic was to make a very easy to use computer language. Many who were using computers in business gravitated toward Basic since it was easy to learn and use. Basic is a very suitable programming language for children to learn on, but it is not nearly as popular as it once was.

As time went on, people who design computer languages and study computer science wanted to be able to better represent objects in the real world. This required them to change the way that computer languages were structured. This led them to create "object-oriented languages." The first of these that was developed is called c++. This became a pretty popular language, and it was based on the older c language, but it can model real-world objects like cars and airplanes (and even people) in computer code that languages like c can't. This language is still pretty popular, but other languages like Java were invented later, in some cases, to help people program the internet.

Python has become one of the most popular programming languages. It is a very simple language, building on the ideas behind the Basic language. However, it's a lot more sophisticated than Basic, and yet it maintains a lot of simplicity. Python is definitely suitable for use by children who are learning how to code. It is freely available for use on most computer systems.

Computer Syntax

No matter what computer language someone settles on to use in order to solve a specific problem, every computer language has its own set of rules for writing out the statements which serve as instructions to the computer. The computer is not going to understand what instructions you give it if they are not written correctly. Computer syntax is a term that refers to the rules for writing the statements given to the computer in the right way. This helps the compiler translate the code without errors. A syntax error occurs when you have mistyped something. There are many ways that this can happen. Obviously, a spelling error can be a cause, but sometimes errors will come about because you are referring to something that the compiler can't find, and this will cause an error because it doesn't recognize a word or name of something.

In the modern age, when there are many libraries and plugins used, referring to something that is missing because the compiler can't locate the source code at the given path is quite common.

The syntax is quite important for the development of computer programs. This can be helpful in training the minds of younger people. Children can learn to focus and be more exact in their writing and other activities by spending time computer programming. The syntax rules are developed so that the compiler can recognize what it is seeing and translate it into machine code that the computer can understand.

Logic Errors

One of the most famous sayings in the computer programming world is garbage-in, garbage-out. It is possible to make errors in a computer program that are syntactically correct, and that also doesn't lead to bugs or crashes. But, they may generate the wrong answers. This can be a problem because these logic errors might be hard to track down or even recognize. Sometimes, the erroneous assumptions that the programmer has in their mind are programmed into the computer.

Programming Mobile/Smart Phones

These days, everyone is interested in learning how to make "apps" for their iPhone or tablet. Children are probably going to be interested in doing this, as smartphones and tablets have become some of the most popular devices used to play games and interact with friends through social media. So, we will take a moment to talk about what programming languages and tools are used to create apps and games for smartphones.

The first major smartphone that became popular was the iPhone. The main tool used to build apps for the iPhone is called XCode. This is free to download, and you can even run apps on a simulator without spending any money. There are many easy to follow tutorials on YouTube that can help children build simple apps and games.

At first, XCode used a very difficult-to-follow language. It was based on the c language and called objective-c. That was a very difficult language for adults and children alike, and it really isn't suitable for children to learn. However, about five years ago, Apple introduced a new programming language they called Swift. The advantage of Swift is that it is much simpler to use and understand. Although programming smartphones can be more complex in some ways, children can learn how to build simple apps using Swift quite easily. One of the benefits of doing this is that children can see their creations come to life, even on a real phone, if you choose to sign up for the Apple developer program. This requires you to pay $100, however, and you must own a Mac computer in order to develop apps for the iPhone and iPad.

For Android phones, there are two tools available. Eclipse is an older software development environment that can be used to develop apps for Android devices. More recently, however, Google has developed its own tool called Android Studio. Both tools use the Java programming language, which does have a bit of sophistication. While it is the opinion of this author that developing simple apps using Swift is possible for children, it's not clear that children will be able to develop

Android apps using these tools. It is just a bit more complicated, although high school-age children may be able to do it in many cases.

There is a tool called Visual Basic for Android that could be considered. This tool uses the simple Basic programming language. It is free to use and also has a simple on-screen designing interface where coders can build their screens for the app visually. They can also build and run their apps on real Android devices if desired. Simulators can also be used.

What Is a Compiler?

A computer cannot understand the high-level languages that have been developed to make coding easier for people. Therefore, for a computer program to actually run on a computer or a smartphone, or on the internet, the program has to be translated into a language that the computer can understand. The only language that the computer can understand is binary, which is the streams of 1's and 0's that make the computer operate the way that it should at each step. There are two ways that a computer program can be converted so that the computer can understand it. The most direct way is by using a compiler.

A compiler is just another computer program. It has one job, and that is to read in the lines of computer code one by one and translate them into 1's and 0's or binary so that the computer can execute the computer code. Often, the resulting translation is stored as a file that is called an executable. The compiler goes through and "compiles" the program, and then writes it to a file that can then be executed.

In the process, the compiler will find many mistakes. These are called errors. A large part of the process of coding will involve resolving all of the errors that are in the computer program that you wrote. This can be a difficult and time-consuming task for large programs. That is one reason that programs are broken down into smaller blocks of code, so you can get each of them working individually, rather than trying to get a very large program working all at once. That makes your work a lot easier.

Interpreters

Some languages are not directly compiled. Instead, they are interpreted. Basic and Python are interpreted. What this means is that each statement is read in when the program is running, and then the interpreter converts that statement into binary language the computer understands. So, it does this while the program is running, line by line. The difference is that a compiler reads in the entire program and writes it to an executable file. When you run the program, the entire program is already translated for the computer. As a result, a compiled program is going to run faster and more efficiently. But in today's world of fast computers, that might not make much difference.

Debugging

When you code, you are going to find that often, if not most of the time, your programs don't work the way you expected. This is because you have some errors in your thought process that were used to build the program in the first place. Errors that happen when the program is actually running are called "bugs." It is claimed that this terminology is used because many years ago, probably in the 1950s, there was a bug inside a computer that was keeping it from running programs the right way. The bug was interfering with the computer's electronics. Sometimes a bug can stop a program from running, and we say that the code has "crashed."

In 2019, we can't be sure if that really happened, but the important part to remember is that few coders get it right the first time. So, don't feel bad if you write some computer code and it doesn't seem to work right. This is an important part of the learning process, and learning how to debug your programs is one of the most important skills that you can learn as you learn how to program computers. This can be very challenging. The first thing to keep in mind is that when your program has a bug in it that is preventing it from operating properly, don't get frustrated and angry. The first step in solving this kind of problem is to note when it occurs. Sometimes it will depend on the type of data that is fed into your code. Some data won't cause the bug, but other data will. So, we need to know about the data the computer is using too if that might be revealing the error. When data causes a bug in your computer code, you have to change your computer code to account for all the data that it might encounter when it runs.

The process of debugging begins by slowly going through your computer code, step by step. You will need to look at each line in your program and follow it along, to find out where the bug is. Then you will have to rewrite the code that caused the program to crash.

Don't let it get you down if you fix the code, and it still crashes. Sometimes fixing a mistake reveals other mistakes. This is just part of the business of coding computers. When you grow up and code for a living, you are going to be doing this kind of work all the time. Even very experienced coders who have been doing it for years have bugs in their programs.

Higher Level Tools

So, we've seen that computer programming can take place on three basic levels. The lowest level is the level of 1's and 0's. That is the language that is easiest for the computer to understand, but hard for people to work with. Then there is assembly language, which is used by engineers that need to be low level, but not quite at the binary level. Finally, there are high-level languages that are used by most coders today, which use English statements to give instructions to the computer.

Some people thought about this and imagined an even better way to do things. They thought, what if you could go to an even higher level? Maybe you could assemble blocks and connect them in a visual way, and not really code at all?

Over the years, several tools have been developed to help people built programs and apps without actually having to do coding. A new layer was added between coding, compiling, and the binary language that the computer understands. And even if you have an iPhone to play your games on, in the end, it is just a computer that understands nothing more than binary.

With a higher-level tool, you can "draw" your program on the screen. Then the tool converts your drawing into code, and then it compiles it. For example, Google has a tool called App Maker that lets people build apps for Android devices without doing much coding. One area where this has really taken off is in the development of video games.

High-Level Tools for Video Games

Video games are one of the easiest ways to get children excited about coding. Since they enjoy playing video games, it's a natural fit for many to want to make them as well. There are many high-level tools for video games that let you draw out the video game on the screen. As you draw out each scene, you can add objects to the scene, exactly as you want them to appear in the game. Then you specify how each object should behave when the game is run.

Several tools are available that are quite similar to scratch in the overall structure and function. They have scenes that can be drawn on screen, and characters and objects can be position and moved around. Then the game designer can set up rules for each of the objects in the scene.

One of the first tools build in this way is called Game Salad. Game Salad is used as an educational tool to help teach children about computer science, and it can be used in a k-12 curriculum. But Game Salad is a real tool, and it can be used to create real games for devices like the iPhone. Game Salad lets you draw the game on the screen, and then set up rules for each object behind the scenes. Game Salad is actually quite similar to scratch, and after a child has mastered scratch, if they are in middle school or high school years using Game Salad will seem like a natural transition.

Another game building tool that some people use is called Corona. It uses a simple programming language call lua. Corona is more coding based than the other tools we are describing in this section; in fact, it is completely coding based. Many people prefer using this method, but these days being able to visualize your scenes and set them up without having to write code is a big step forward that saves a lot of work. That also helps the game developer focus on the actual design of the game itself, while with Lua, they are going to be getting lost in the coding details just to position objects on the screen and have them move about.

After Game Salad, more sophisticated game building tools were developed that are visually oriented. Buildbox is a very easy tool to use that is excellent for children. They can learn how to create games without coding at all, but they can also use "scripts" to specialize the code behind the scenes for their own games. Buildbox has been used to develop some of the most frequently downloaded apps on the Apple app store. A game is divided into a series of scenes, and you design each scene as if you were using PowerPoint or Keynote, specifying the properties of each object on the scene. It then compiles it into a working game for you. Buildbox comes in 2D and 3D versions. When using the 2D version, ordinary graphics can be imported into the development environment to set up backgrounds, characters, objects, and enemies. The design can actually get quite sophisticated using logic tools, and many different templates can help the designer build game mechanics that are similar to many successful chart-topping games.

The 3D version of the buildbox is a little more sophisticated. Since it's a true 3D system, the objects in the games are actually meshes rather than image files. This version of buildbox also lets designers get under the hood. Mind maps let you build up the behaviors of characters and other objects in the game, and you can actually work with the coding scripts of each element in the mind map. Those who master coding will be able to take advantage of these features in order to build up more sophisticated and complex games.

Unity 3D is the most sophisticated and popular tool used to build games for multiple platforms, including mobile, tablets, desktop computers, Apple TV, and Xbox. Unity is a middle ground tool, you build scenes visually on the screen, and set properties, but it also has coding behind it using a derivative of the c programming language called c# (c sharp). Unity developers are in high demand by the video gaming industry, so any children who are interested in careers as video game programmers can benefit by learning unity, once they have learned to code very well in other contexts. Unity is powerful but a bit complicated. However, older children can begin learning Unity by following a careful course.

Language Tools Everyone Should Know

You can take this section with a little bit of a grain of salt. The reason I say that is computer languages are constantly evolving, and preferences and fads can come and go. That said, there are some core fundamental languages that should be learned at more advanced ages if the child is hoping to have some kind of career as a computer programmer or scientist.

The first is c++. This was probably the first object-oriented programming language, and it is still widely used. There are some aspects of the language that make it hard to learn for some people, but the advantage of learning it is that not only will you gain a valuable skill that is still used in a wide range of applications, it serves as a solid training ground that makes picking up other computer languages quite easy.

Java is also good to know. This is a language that is used in a lot of different applications, and its offshoot JavaScript is often used in web programming. Java was chosen as the language for apps made for the Android operating system, so knowing it is certainly going to be useful for job prospects since so many companies want to make Android apps.

Python is a great language to learn. The great thing about python is that it's simple. It may be the simplest programming language that you can learn. After a child masters scratch, learning python is a definite next step. Furthermore, it's available on every computer system. If you have a Mac or a PC, you can get python, and it might already be installed on your computers. You can learn all of the important concepts of computer programming using python, including classes, lists, subroutines, functions, and more.

Ruby is a very popular programming language in the business world. It is one of the younger languages, C and C++ were developed long before Ruby came on the scene. Like python, ruby is considered easy to learn and use. Ruby can be used in a wide range of circumstances, including programming on the internet. This wide applicability is one thing that has generated a lot of its popularity. Ruby has been the backbone of many popular social media sites.

Finally, learning swift, which is now the standard language for Apple apps for the iPhone, is a definite skill that children who are interested in becoming coders should learn. The beauty of swift is that it's one of the easiest coding languages to learn.

Career options

There is a wide range of career options. In the following sections, we will go over some of them.

Coding as Engineering

Computer programming is used extensively in almost any engineering setting. Whether you are working on optics, medical devices, or weapons, coding is an important skill that is used in virtually any industry. Automobiles are becoming more computerized and sophisticated. Computer programmers can build software for testing, to run systems in the cars themselves, or in simulators to test new designs and investigate safety features. Computer programmers are working in manufacturing and other areas, involved in everything from scheduling to controlling robotics and other critical tasks.

Data Science

Data science is a truly modern interdisciplinary field. We've heard a lot of hype about this kind of job, and it's finally arrived. Data science involves computer science, using machine learning and artificial intelligence, statistics, and business acumen. Data science doesn't use direct coding very much, but the skills learned while coding can help the data scientist do their job. A data scientist must use discernment to train artificially intelligent computer systems on how to perform their tasks. The work data scientists are doing is having a huge impact on the business world. For example, Southwest Airlines claims that machine learning managed by their data science team saved them hundreds of millions of dollars in expenses related to fuel costs. The way to get into data science is probably by majoring in computer science in college and taking a lot of statistics courses. Any child that chooses to go into this field is going to have a very secure career path. This is definitely a job that is just now coming into its own, and it's a job that is going to last going forward. Data scientists are involved in many game-changing research projects like self-driving vehicles and providing internet security against hacking and fraud.

Coding for Business

Coders are needed for any type of business or large organization, such as a hospital. Anywhere computers are used – which is virtually everywhere these days – is somewhere that might need a lot of computer programmers. The type of work done is quite varied but can include database management, or more sophisticated tasks like writing code to control Lasik machines. It is impossible to list all of the possible ways that computer programmers are used in business. But one thing we can be sure of is the demand for computer programmers in business is something that is going to keep increasing in the coming decades.

Coding for Finance

The introduction of computers to the world of finance has brought computer programming along with it in unexpected ways. There are many opportunities to write software for hedge funds, stock market trading floors, and stockbrokers.

Coding for the Government

Governments of all levels are always hiring computer programmers. At the federal level, you can work directly for any government agency, or you can work as an independent contractor and command a high salary. The department of defense and department of energy hire computer coders to do a lot of important work for national security that pays very well. Many government agencies are hiring experts in cybersecurity, and becoming a coder is one way to get into this field. Smaller government agencies also hire many coders to do all types of work, such as working with large databases they use in the course of their usual work. As time goes on, the need for these experts is only going to increase, so it is a good bet as a career path going into the future.

Coding as a Business

Coding can also be a lucrative choice for self-employment. This can be done on many levels. For example, you can set up a consulting business that is hired by others when they need coding done, but they don't want to have in house programmers. This can be a very high paying career choice if you know how to sell yourself and get started. It is probably a good idea to get some work experience in the employ of others before you try getting clients as an independent programmer because people are going to want some kind of track record before they are going to make that kind of commitment to hiring you.

Designing mobile apps and websites for people is also an option for those who want to pursue coding as a business. Although the app stores have matured, there is still a rush to get large numbers of apps on the app stores. People have app ideas that they don't know how to implement, and those who are not inclined to program computers themselves are often willing to pay top dollar to hire others to do the work for them. In addition to making apps, many businesses will hire independent agencies to make websites for them. This can include the maintenance of large databases.

Besides making programs for others, it is possible to use coding to build your own app business. You can sell software that you have developed as desktop applications, or as mobile apps. This is a very competitive business, so it's not something to look at with rose-colored glasses. However, it is possible to have some success doing this, and those who succeed usually end up being very successful.

There are many options

As you can see, there are many options available for those who are interested in coding for a living. If your child finds coding interesting, they are not going to go wrong by picking it as a career option. They can either go forward working for someone else, including a large corporation, smaller business, or government agency. Or they can consult or start their own business.

Conclusion

I want to thank you for taking the time to read this book! I certainly hope that you have found it informative and useful. The goal in this book was to keep things simple so that beginners can understand scratch and get started with using it, but hopefully, we've kept it interesting and fun as well.

Coding is a challenging and fun career, and since society is getting more dependent on computers and networks, the need for coders is only going to increase. Of course, even if your child is not going to be a coder, they can still benefit in many ways from learning some coding. First off, coding helps to train the mind to think carefully. Coding will help your child learn how to focus on and complete things that they have started. One lesson that all parents should strive for is making sure that children complete the projects that they start at scratch. This alone is a skill worth learning, even if they don't continue to code later.

Coding will also help children develop skills in logical thinking. You don't have to be a math whiz to do basic coding, but learning to code is going to improve the math skills of anyone who learns it and help them to think logically.

The go-to website for scratch is run by MIT, and it can be found here: https://scratch.mit.edu/

The best approach to use is to find simple tasks on the site, but tasks that are also interesting. One task that is good to try is one we touched on in the book. That is the animated letters. This is a fun task that children enjoy, and it lets them directly connect the commands they are giving the computer to the action that they see on the screen. The animation process can also involve several different methods, and so it also gives the children a chance to learn a lot about scratch, in a simple context.

There are many other good lessons to learn. However, if you are browsing around the MIT site, you are going to find that many of the projects posted on the site are quite sophisticated. Many of these have been developed by scratch fans in the general public. They can be instructive later, but they may not be suitable for beginners. The worst thing that can be done is intimidating a child by having them encounter codes that are complicated, and when they are just starting out, they may find that overwhelming. It will destroy the child's confidence. The site does provide many beginners tutorials. You can rely on those until the child has gained some experience. Then they can learn more complex programs that will take a longer time to figure out.

When guiding your children with scratch, it is important not to force them to do it. Not everyone is going to be inclined to do computer programming. If some children find it uninteresting, let them try something else. It is not going to be the end of the world if your child does not grow up to be a coder.

Again, thank you for reading my book. Please drop by Amazon and leave a thoughtful review, we'd love to hear how the book is helping you and your children!

Python For Kids

The New Step By Step Parent-Friendly Programming Guide With Detailed Installation Instruction To Stimulate Your Kid With Awesome Games, Activities And Projects

Introduction

This book is intended for children who wish to learn to program especially Python. In this day and age, computer knowledge, or literacy, if we may call it that, is of huge importance for every person, from early childhood on through to his or her adult, professional lives. Even in the preschool system, children very often have tasks given to them by their teachers, which require the use of computers to a certain extent. That is precisely the reason this book would be of good use both for teachers and for children. Teachers will get help on the topic of how to bring the computer closer to children, and children get the opportunity to learn their first basic knowledge of computers and their use. They also get their first clues on the benefits computers can bring to them and their lives. For example, from an early age, children learn to explore using computers. In this way, their curiosity and exploring skills rise, which can later help them through the school system, and in their lives as adult working people, because today, there is no profession not related to computers in some way. From surgeons, who use the latest technologies when operating and saving human lives, to the astronauts who use highly sophisticated computerized equipment when preparing to go to space.

Technological developments in the last two decades have enabled us to have great things. These developments have made our lives much easier but also much faster-paced than ever before. Things have gotten so hectic lately that we have to carry loads of information with us wherever you go, from the earliest stages of our lives. Today, almost every child carries a cell phone or a tablet everywhere, and within that tablet or phone lays a huge amount of all kinds of data, from their contacts to e-books to video games. This means that technology has "taken over" every single sphere of our life: from work and driving automated cars filled with electronic and automatic devices, to our free time, which most of us spend in front of a computer or other device playing games or posting and chatting on social media sites. Even before starting school, our children learn the basics of operating a computer. They have to, because, even in the preschool system they are required to use computers. This is because they have to be prepared for the first school day when they are going to enter a classroom full of computers and other equipment, which they will have to be able to use if they want to keep up with the other students in a class.

For all the reasons mentioned above, "Python for Kids" is intended to be a useful book for children and parents alike, and to serve as a guide into taking the first steps to learn python programming. Teachers get an idea of how to approach children when teaching them the python program, and children get acquainted with how the programs that they use are made, and on how they can make programs of their own that can and will be useful to them. This should also enhance their creativity and imagination, which is of crucial importance to their growth and development in childhood, as well as for their lives as adult people. If they decide to go "in-depth," children can learn how to do something more, beyond the simplistic. The scope of interest in learning computer science depends on the needs and interests of each individual, child, or adult alike. If programming is presented to them in a way that sparks their interest and curiosity, then the kids will start exploring the world of computers, always searching for something new and exciting they can make themselves.

As the computer world is very advanced and fast-paced, new solutions for a particular problem appear every day. This means that kids interested in computers have to follow the innovations and news in the field they want to explore further, no matter what it is. For example, if they are interested in making video games (which most kids initially use the computer for, even before they are old enough to start preschool education) they constantly have to follow computer science news or the innovations in the computing field they are interested in, programming languages, and updates to programs and languages used to create computer programs and applications. Imagine you have coded a calendar. The basic one, where you have 12 months and 365 days and just a small space next to each day where you can note your appointments and tasks for that day. This is good for today, but as soon as tomorrow comes, a program with more advanced functions will appear on the market. Someone else has found a way to put, for example, more space for editing next to each day, or a clock is coded into the calendar. In this new, advanced calendar, besides the date, you can keep track of time during each day--or perhaps holidays are now included, or the ability to set audible reminders in the calendar. This is the kind of innovation we are talking about in this book. That is why you need to follow your chosen field very closely. Every day you may see and learn new things, which were not available yesterday. For some kids (actually, for most of them) always being better at doing and creating things presents a challenge. In the modern world, things move along and progress quickly. The world itself became fast-paced. So, you have to follow the trends and stay up to date to be successful in anything you do, whether it is computer science or something else entirely. Everything is now computer-based and so, you have to keep track of technological innovations daily if you want to keep up with the rest of the world.

The computer world is very competitive in the so-called "fun" part of the field, too. This means that programmers are always coming up with something new for their end-users. For example, it is a matter of prestige to create games with better graphics, more colors, options, more gaming characters (if the game theme is character-based such as fighting games are). Nowadays, many children show interest in programming from an early age, and, as computer knowledge is very useful, in this way they make a good head start for themselves pretty early on in life. Some preschool institutions in Serbia and in many preschools around the world have some sort of computing class or coursework integrated within their educational plan. This means that computing, or computer science, as it is known, is of critical importance and, therefore, we need to learn the basics of it from early childhood on forward. Whether for playing games or constructing a small program of their own, computers are now a daily presence in almost every child's life.

Programming also enhances logical reasoning skills, because, for even the simplest programming task, the use of logic is essential. Furthermore, this logical way of thinking is good for developing children's math and science skills. Programming and the use of computers is also a science in itself.

The reasons mentioned here make programming one of the most useful and beneficial skills for both children and adults alike to possess. As with most other science-based disciplines, it is best to start learning early in childhood - the sooner, the better. Therefore, this book is written to motivate children to start learning to code to enhance their imaginations and logic skills, and to prepare them for their future adult lives. Today, computer literacy is mandatory. This book can help you give the children in your life the tools they need to be successful when they are grown.

Chapter 1

What is Coding?

Coding is the process of putting together the segments of your data that seem to illustrate an idea or concept. In this way, coding is a way of making abstractions from the existing data in their resources to build a greater understanding of the forces involved.

Remember that it is possible to code any portion of the content of a resource on any number of nodes to show that it is related to each of its concepts or categories.

Why do you need to code your resources?

The coding of the content of your resources can contribute significantly to your analysis in several ways:

- Coding generates ideas while codifying the material of its resources. It is possible to interpret passages and discover new meanings in the data.

- Coding allows you to gather and view all the material related to a category or case through all its resources. Viewing all this material allows you to review the coded segments in context and create new and more refined categories as you gain a new understanding of the meaning of the data.

- The codification of its resources facilitates the search for patterns and theories. It is possible to browse the encoded content of your resources using queries and search functionality to test theories and find new patterns in your data.

Example: When coding in C the algorithm of the program Add, seen in the Design, something similar to:

```
#include <stdio.h>

int main ()

{

    int a, b, c;

    printf ("\ n first n% number (integer):", 163);

    scanf ("% d", & a);

    printf ("\ n second n% number (integer):", 163);

    scanf ("% d", & b);

    c = a + b;

    printf ("\ n The sum is:% d", c);

    return 0;
```

To encode an algorithm you have to know the syntax of the language to which it will be translated. However, regardless of the programming language in which a program is written, it will be its algorithm that determines its logic. The logic of a program establishes what its actions are and in what order they should be executed. Therefore, it is convenient for every programmer to learn to design algorithms before moving on to the coding phase.

Programming languages

A programming language can be defined as an artificial language that allows you to write the instructions of a computer program or put another way. A programming language allows the programmer to communicate with the computer to tell it what it has to do. Many programming languages have invented by man. We can classify into three main types: **the machine**, **low level**, and **high level**.

Machine language is the only one that understands the digital computer. it is its "natural language". Only two symbols can be used on it: zero (0) and one (1). Therefore, machine language is also called binary language. The computer can only work with bits. However, it is not easy for the programmer to write instructions such as:

10100010
11110011
00100010
00010010

For this reason, more understandable programming languages were invented for the programmer.

Thus, **low-level** languages appeared, also called assembly languages, which allow the programmer to write the instructions of a program using English abbreviations, also called mnemonic words, such as ADD, DIV, SUB, etc., instead of use zeros and ones. For example, the instruction:

ADD a, b, c

It could be the translation of the action:

c ← a + b

This action is present in the Add algorithm of the Design, which indicated that in the memory space represented by the variable c the sum of the two numbers stored in the memory spaces represented by the variables a and b must be stored.

A program written in an assembly language has the disadvantage that it is not understandable to the computer since it is not composed of zeros and ones. To translate the instructions of a program written in an assembly language to instructions of a machine language, you must use a program called an assembler.

An added difficulty to binary languages is the fact that they are dependent on the machine, or rather, the processor, that is, each processor uses a different machine language, a different set of instructions, which is defined in its hardware. Consequently, a program written for a type of processor cannot be used on other equipment that uses a different processor, since the program will not be portable. For this program to work on a second computer, all instructions written in the machine language of the first computer must be translated into the binary language of the second computer, which is a very expensive and complex job for the programmer.

Likewise, since the instructions that can be written in an assembly language are always associated with the binary instructions of a particular computer, assembly languages are also processor dependent. However, high-level languages are independent of the processor, that is, a program written on any computer with high-level language can be transported to any other computer, with small changes or even none.

A high-level language allows the programmer to write the instructions of a program using words or syntactic expressions. For example, in C you can use words such as case, if, for, while, etc. to build with the instructions like:

> if ($n^0 > 0$) printf ("The number% is positive", 163);

This translated into Spanish comes to say that, if the number is greater than zero, then write the message on the screen: "The number is positive."

Another important feature of high-level languages is that, for most of the instructions in these languages, several instructions in an assembly language would be needed to indicate the same. In the same way that, most of the instructions of an assembly language, also groups several instructions of a machine language.

On the other hand, a program is written in a high-level language also does not get rid of the inconvenience of the fact that it is not understandable to the computer and, therefore, to translate the instructions of a program written in a high-level language to instructions of a machine language, you have to use another program that is called a compiler.

Compilers and interpreters

The instruction set written in a high-level language is called the source code of the program. Thus, the compiler is a program that receives as input data the source code of a program written by a programmer and generates as output a set of instructions written in the binary language of the computer where they will be executed. The set of instructions generated by the compiler is called the object code of the program, also known as machine code or binary code, since it is, in itself, a program executable by the machine.

Normally, a C programmer will use an editing program to write the source code of a program, and save it in a file with the extension (.c); for example, "Add.c". Next, a C compiler will translate the source code into object code, saving it with another extension, which, depending on the operating system may vary. For example, in Windows, it will be saved with the extension (.obj), short for the object.

On the other hand, there is a type of program called interpreter, which also serves to translate the source code of a program into object code, but its way of acting is different from that of a compiler.

The operation of an interpreter is characterized by translating and executing, one by one, the instructions of the source code of a program, but without generating as output object code. The process performed by an interpreter is as follows: read the first instruction of the source code, translate it into object code and execute it; then do the same with the second instruction; and so on, until you reach the last instruction of the program, as long as there is no error that stops the process. In a program, there can be three types of errors: syntax, execution, and logic.

Types of errors

When a syntax error exists in any instruction of the source code of a program, this error will prevent both the compiler and the interpreter from translating said instruction, since neither of them will understand what the programmer is telling you. For example, if instead of the instruction:

> printf ("\ n first n% number (integer):", 163);

A programmer writes:

```
prrintf ("\ n first n% number (integer):", 163);
```

When the compiler or the interpreter reads this line of code, neither of them will understand what prrintf is and, therefore, they will not know how to translate this instruction into machine code, therefore, both will stop the translation and notify the programmer with a message of error.

In summary, syntax errors are detected in the process of translating the source code into binary code. On the contrary that it happens with the errors of execution and of logic that can only be detected when the program is running.

A runtime error occurs when the computer cannot execute any instructions correctly. For example, the instruction:

```
c = 5/0;
```

It is syntactically correct and will be translated into binary code. However, when the computer tries to perform the division:

```
5/0
```

An execution error will occur, since, mathematically, it cannot be divided by zero.

As for logic errors, they are the most difficult to detect. When a program has no syntax or execution errors but still does not work well, this is due to the existence of some logical error. So, a logic error occurs when the results obtained are not as expected. For example, if instead of the instruction:

```
c = a + b;
```

A programmer would have written:

```
c = a * b;
```

Until the result of the operation was shown on the screen, the programmer could not realize the error, provided he already knew the result of the sum in advance. In this case, the programmer could easily notice the error, but, when the operations are more complex, the logic errors can be very difficult to detect.

What can you make with code?

You can do many things with codes. For example, let's see what can be done with JavaScript code.

The things that can be done with Code are very varied, among the most prominent are:

1. You can obtain the information about the browser that the user is using, the version of it, the operating system on which it is running, and even the screen resolution that you have configured on your computer.

2. You can work with pop-up and interactive dialogs created with div elements, instead of pop-up windows, which have stopped being used for security and design reasons.

3. You can create sophisticated menu systems with pop-up submenus that are activated with the user action.

4. Values entered in form fields can be validated before they are sent to the server.

5. You can create navigation trees to make it easier for users to move from one page to another through your website.

6. You can create substitution effects for images controlled by the action of placing or removing the mouse pointer.

7. You can create some animations such as transitions of images and objects from a web page.

8. You can change the position of HTML elements on the web page dynamically or controlled by the movement of the mouse pointer.

9. You can redirect the user from one page to another, without the need for a static link.

10. You can perform some calculations with the values entered in the form fields.

11. You can get the date of the operating system where the web page is running on the client.

12. Sophisticated calendar controls can be created to select a date, instead of being manually entered by users in form fields.

Chapter 2

Python Theory

When talking about Python theory, Artificial Learning, Deep Learning, and Machine Learning will be discussed because these three will let you understand Python. As such, we will steer the direction of our discussion towards discerning whether the difference between these three types of learning is evidently pronounced or just subtle. The diagram below depicts the relationship between Artificial Intelligence (Artificial Learning), Machine Learning, and Deep Learning.

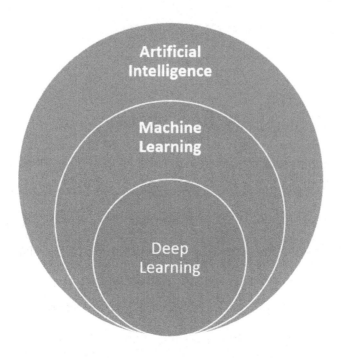

Artificial Intelligence

Let's discuss Artificial Intelligence first. Artificial Intelligence is basically referred to as the development of an Artificial Intelligence System all by itself, imitating the learning pattern of human beings. In other words, A.I is a computer system that can harness the human learning prowess and perform tasks without any output from human operators. Artificial Intelligence is actually a scientific endeavor that was pioneered by a handful of computer scientists back in the 1950s, and the main goal of this endeavor is to enable computers to automate all those tasks which are by nature, intellectual, and performed by humans. Hence, due to the nature of Artificial Intelligence, it encompasses Machine Learning as well as Deep Learning, along with many other techniques and approaches which don't involve any learning whatsoever. The field and concept of A.I is still largely unexplored even after so many years of its introduction because of modern hardware limitations. However, this does not insinuate that Artificial Intelligence is just pure science fiction; on the contrary, A.I has many promising prospects and is currently a field of extensive research and experimentation.

Machine Learning

The concept of machine learning goes far back to the early 19th century when the advent of the first general-purpose computer, the "Analytical Engine," was realized. Although this machine wasn't meant as a "general-purpose computer" because the very concept of general computation was not present at the time. Hence, the major purpose of this machine was to be a tool that could automate certain computations in mathematical analysis. Due to this, the machine was given the name of "Analytical Engine." Now the reason we are discussing such an early invention is because of a remark made by a certain lady on this very machine. The name of this woman was Lady Ada Lovelace, and she was an acquaintance and a collaborator of the inventor of the Analytical Engine, Charles Babbage. The main idea of the remark was that the Analytical Engine was just a piece of machinery that could only assist us in matters which we already know of and just automate some mathematical functions and calculations through our input.

The reason why this remark is so important in the history of Machine Learning is that the pioneer of Artificial Intelligence, Alan Turing quoted Lady Ada Lovelace's remark as a "Lady Ada Lovelace's objection," in his paper when he introduced the Turing Test for the first time. He concluded that general-purpose machines (computers) did have the potential for originality and learning, much like human beings.

We have briefly discussed some boring and seemingly irrelevant history of a general-purpose computer. Still, it is quite the contrary, the very concept of Machine Learning arises from this question that we have just outlined and that question is this:

"Is it possible for a computer to perform a task or solve a problem in a way that is beyond what we know and also learn to perform certain specific tasks independently without any human input?

Is it possible for a computer, a machine made by humans, and programmed by humans with functioning that is pre-determined and predicted to surprise us? Instead of being inputted with rules of data-processing by programmers, is a computer capable of just looking at the sample data and learning the rules by itself?

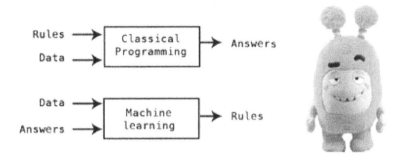

These very questions have brought into existence an entirely new and ambitiously unique programming paradigm. To get a better understanding of the potentials of Machine Learning, let's make a simple contrast between the working of an A.I system and a Machine Learning system on data-processing. In a system using Artificial Intelligence (symbolic A.I), the user basically inputs a program that contains specific rules for data processing. Then data is introduced, which is to be processed according to the specified rules. Hence we obtain a result showing us the answers. However, in a Machine Learning system, we do not provide the rules. Instead, the system is given the data as well as a result (answers), which are expected from this sample data. The Machine Learning system then proceeds to infer and learn the rules through which the corresponding result can be obtained. Once the system has learned the rules, it can be applied to new data and produce entirely original results.

To sum it up, the major feature which distinguishes Machine Learning from Artificial Intelligence is that the former is systematically trained rather than being explicitly programmed, as is the case in Artificial Intelligence. So, a system using Machine Learning is simply given a bundle of examples that are relevant to the primary task. The system then figures out the underlying statistical structure of these examples and then figures out the rules governing the end results of these examples. Once the system has learned the rules, corresponding tasks can now be automated by the system.

In conclusion, Machine Learning is a sub-field of Artificial Intelligence that gained popularity and flourished ever since the 1990s to this day. As new computer hardware started to be developed and existing technologies saw major upgrades and improvements, a trend has been set for faster hardware and larger datasets paving the way for exploring more possibilities in Machine Learning. Machine Learning, along with Deep Learning, is more focused on being practical rather than theoretical as very little mathematical theory is involved. Hence, this discipline is geared towards proving ideas empirically rather than theoretically.

Deep Learning

Just as how Machine Learning is a sub-field of Artificial Intelligence, similarly, Deep Learning is a sub-field of Machine Learning. The primary aspect which sets the two apart is that Deep Learning employs an entirely new learning representation from data. Deep Learning majorly emphasizes the idea of successive layers in a data sample, which gives a model of increasingly meaningful representations. In other words, this learning model takes into account the multiple layers of data representation while analyzing the sample. In addition, there is another terminology used for the data sample in Deep Learning, known as the "depth of the model," this basically refers to the number of layers that are contributing to a model of the data.

Today, the Deep Learning system uses models of data which consist of tens to thousands of successive layers of representation. This widens the scope of the system as it can handle the learning process involving so many layers. On the other hand, Machine Learning often uses learning approaches which only involve one or two layer of representations of data (due to which they are termed as shallow learning).

To further understand Deep Learning, we need to understand the mechanism through which the system actually "learns," and this learning is done through networks that are structured in such a way that they have layers piled upon one another. This network is known as a neural network. It is also important to clear a major misunderstanding that Deep Learning imitates the working of our brain. While it is true that the neural network used in Deep Learning does draw some inspiration from the human brain, but that is the extent of it. On the contrary, Deep Learning is essentially a mathematical framework that is designed to learn representations from data. Neural Networks have no relevance to the concepts described in Neurobiology, and hence, associating Deep Learning to it would mislead the general masses.

We have been discussing the layers of representations from data, however, to reinforce our understanding of this concept, we will proceed to examine how a neural network of a Deep Learning system learns to recognize and distinguish a digit. An image first represents the digit, and this image is then transformed into a different form of representation when passed through each successive layer as shown below:

In other words, the original image has been converted into representations that are entirely different from the original image. Hence, we can consider the Neural Network of a Deep Learning system as a distilling apparatus that distills information through a multi-stage process to produce a concentrated representation of the sample data, as shown below in detail.

Chapter 3

Welcome to Python!

In this day and age, programming has become nearly as essential as learning how to read and write. It is a valuable skill that anyone can use, even if they aren't programmers. For instance, a boring task like sending emails with news updates and company business updates can easily be automated through the power of coding. There is no need to perform boring tasks manually when a simple program can be written to do the work for you. This is why learning how to program is so important. It can help anyone no matter where they are in life.

The good news is, learning how to program isn't even as difficult as many like to believe. Everyone can learn how to program in any language. That's right, no matter your age and your schooling, you can learn how to code. Children don't need to be "talented", or have some special skills in mathematics in order to get started. The entire world is being digitized and automated. Not learning how to code in the next decade will most likely leave a young person with a serious disadvantage in life, but fortunately, it is really simple to get started.

Learning how to program has never been easier. Nowadays, every company and organization requires some level of programming or interaction with technology. But programming isn't just a useful tool, it is also fun! Coding is all about the ability to solve problems. It is about researching, brainstorming, and fitting the puzzle pieces together. It can even be about art and creativity. Many programmers, myself included, have built a passion for programming due to the ability to create fun games! Your child can easily learn to direct his or her creativity into creating a whole new world, with a story, and interesting scenarios. Many programmers choose the artistic route because they need to explore their creativity.

But what about applications? Aren't they far more complex? The answer is no! Mobile apps, games, fancy software, they all rely on the same concepts we are going to explore in this book. It is easy to encourage your child to have fun with technology and create something, because all it takes understands the building blocks well enough to place them in a certain order, often creative.

In addition to all of the aforementioned benefits, programming is often a group activity. Whether creating applications or games, your child will have the chance to interact and socialize with other likeminded children. There are many online groups, programming clubs, online academies, and other social channels where your child will be able to learn with others how to solve problems, create something out of nothing, and above all make some new friends.

With that being said, in this chapter we are going to start our journey by learning all the basics. So let's get started and explore the wonderful world of programming by first learning the basics.

The Best Starting Point

Python is a programming language that is recommended to children and beginners in particular for one simple reason. It is the most easy to read and understand language out there because of its similarity to written English. While other languages may have some unordinary keywords or a seemingly strange syntax, Python is as close to English as it gets. Here's a simple example using the traditional first program that every beginner writes when barely starting out:

print ("Hello, world!")

As you can see, you don't need any programming knowledge to understand what's going on. It's so simple even a child can understand this line without knowing anything about coding. We'll talk more about what's happening in this simple program later. For now, you and your child should know that Python is much easier to read and write than other more sophisticated programming languages. This example, although extremely rudimentary, is no different from the more complex programs written in Python. They will simply be collections of lines of code similar to the one above. With that being said, let's see the other reasons why your child should start out with Python instead of other languages and why you should encourage their interests early on.

Python is intuitive: We already talked about this briefly, but it can't be said often enough. Python reads like plain English. That is why even elementary schools and high schools are starting to implement Python programming into their curriculum. Python is the perfect language to get kids interested in coding because it allows them to turn their creative ideas into tangible results on the computer screen. They can imagine a program or a game and then simply write it using some basic logic. In addition, Python involves a lot less lines of code necessary to take a certain action. For instance, Java and C++, although industry standards and very popular programming languages, require a lot more steps to perform an action. That means that a child would have to struggle more to write down the same idea, and that can easily build up frustration. What we want is for the child to have fun while learning because that will drive him even more. Python simply makes sense and it allows children to focus on learning how to think logically and how to solve problems, instead of fighting complex coding syntax.

Python is accessible: Another major advantage is the fact that Python is easy to install at home and it is freely available. Python doesn't require a license; therefore you don't need to pay anything to use it. It is available through an open source license, meaning that anyone can use it whether for education or even commercially. You are even allowed to write your own Python distributions and libraries and then sell them, even though they are still similar to the official release. Who knows, maybe your kid will hit it big, and it won't even cost him or her anything. While on the financial topic, you as a parent should also know that you don't need any kind of fancy tech to install Python. All you need is a desktop or laptop computer, and it doesn't matter what operating system it's running. Whether you have a machine that works with Windows, Linux, or Mac, you can install Python just as easily on all three. All you need to do is visit the official page, download Python and follow the installation process.

Python helps with child development: Python or programming in general, isn't only for those who are determined to pursue a career in computer science or game development. Programming can help a child develop problem solving skills that are so crucial in our daily lives. Furthermore, it helps them develop the ability to think critically. But the benefits don't stop there. Even if you think your child may not be interested in programming or mathematics later in life, learning how to program will help him or her to develop skills in writing and thinking creatively as well. It's all due to the fact that your child will have to combine critical thinking with creativity in order to solve problems when creating programs or games. This combination between logic and creativity will have a powerful impact no matter what the child will choose to do in later years.

Python is here to stay: Python has established itself as one of the best languages not just for beginners, but for industry experts as well. For instance, Python is also used in computer science, analytics, machine learning, artificial intelligence development, robotics and a lot more. It is a powerful, versatile and efficient language that can be used with anything, and it can be later combined with other more complex programming languages like C++. Because of these points, Python is quite future proof, and even ten to twenty years from now your child may still be working with Python. As mentioned earlier, Python today is used behind some of the most powerful technologies and corporations in the world. Amazon, Google, Facebook, NASA, YouTube and many more rely on Python. Because the language is such a core element of all of these big names, it will not go away any time soon. And even if somehow Python would disappear into the void, it is so easy to transfer to another programming language when you have already mastered one. For instance, most people who are experts in Python can become proficient programmers in other languages like C# or JavaScript within weeks, not years.

If you are still not sure whether Python is the right starting point for your child, there are other alternatives. Perhaps your child is still too young, or you are worried that focusing on the language's syntax may prove to be too challenging and frustrating. That is not a problem! If your child is too young for a fully featured programming language, you might want to look into an alternative such as Scratch. Scratch is something known as a visual, block-based programming language developed by MIT and aimed purely at children with the purpose of introducing them to the world of programming. All the user needs to do is head to the official website, and use a block-like user interface to create any project.

This alternative cannot be called a proper programming language becomes it is not fully customizable by the programmer and it is limited when it comes to complex projects. However, it is aimed at children above the age of 8, and because of its visual focus your child can purely focus on developing his or her creativity and problem solving skills without worrying about programming theory and coding syntax. The creators of Scratch have realized that the skills needed to code computer applications have become an important aspect of literacy. Therefore, this alternative to Python still pushes the child to design projects, solve problems, and share ideas with a vast online community.

In this book, however, we will focus on Python, but you should still look into Scratch as a simple online, readily available alternative if you think it would be better as a starting point. Once your child grows out of Scratch, Python will be there waiting to stimulate his or her creativity and way of thinking even more.

Now, let's get back to Python and start installing it on your computer.

Chapter 4

Step-by-step and must know

On a pc

If you are using Windows machine, you can follow the procedure below.

Step1. Let us begin by opening up our web browser and going straight to the source. In the address bar, type in www.python.org and you will be greeted by a simplistic website as shown here:

Step2. Mouse cursor over 'Downloads' and the website should be able to detect your platform and present the corresponding version accordingly automatically.

Step3. Click on the button to commence the download.

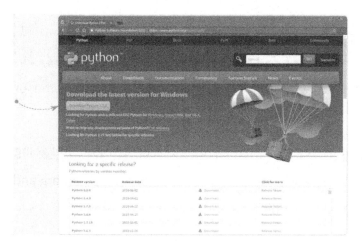

Step4. Once your download is complete, click on it to begin installation. There will be a pop up window.

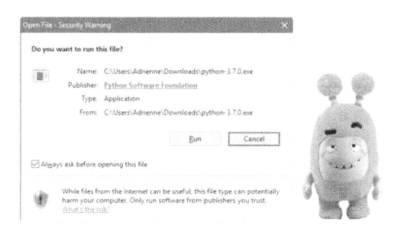

Step5. After download and installation you can simply run the downloaded file, by double-clicking on the Python file. A dialog box will appear that looks like this:

Step6. Make sure the check the ADD PYTHON 3.7 TO PATH checkbox.

Step7. Then just click Install Now. Python will begin installation. A pop up Window below will appear.

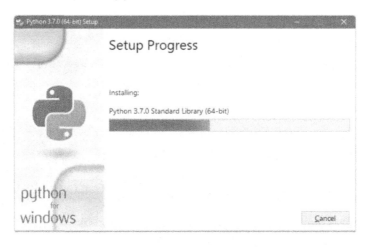

Step8. A few minutes later you should have a working Python installed on your system.

Step9. Yehey! You're done installing and you are ready to start your python journey on windows!

On Mac

Step1. On your computer, open an Internet browser like Google Chrome or Mozilla Firefox.

Step2. In the address bar, type "https://www.python.org/downloads/" to go to the official Python website's Downloads section.

Step3. Through the magic of coding, the website will probably know what type of computer you are using, and the DOWNLOAD button will show you the correct version of Python to install! In our case, we want the latest version, which was Python 3.7.0. Don't worry if it tells you to download a newer version. You can also find the installer for your specific machine in the Files section.

Step4. After clicking on the version, a download should start. Wait for it to finish before starting the installer.

Step5. When you start the installer, you should see a window like this one:

Step6. Click the CONTINUE button. You'll then be presented with some important information that you can choose to read or not.

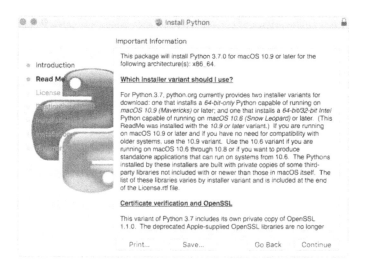

Step7. Click the CONTINUE button. Next you will see the license information.

Step8. Click the CONTINUE button. You'll be asked to agree to the terms of the software license agreement.

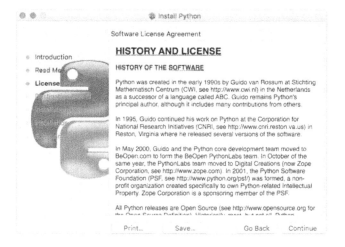

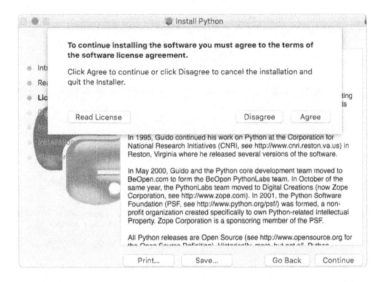

Step9. Click the AGREE button. You'll reach this final window:

Step10. Click the INSTALL button. If you need to, enter your personal user name and password for your account on your computer. Mac OS sometimes asks for this to make sure you want to install something. If you don't see this pop-up window, you can skip to the next step.

Step11. Installation should begin.

Step12. Wait for the installation to finish. Once it is done, you should see this:

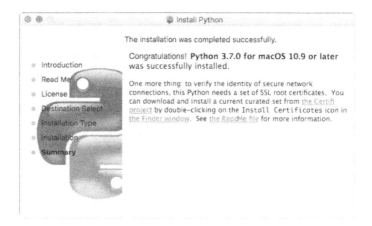

Step 14. Congratulate yourself! You've just installed Python on your Mac!

Using idle

When you download and install Python, it will also install an application called IDLE. Integrated Development and Learning Environment or also known as IDLE, it is an integrated development environment, or IDE, that helps us with writing Python programs. Think of it as an electronic notepad with some additional tools to help us write, debug, and run our Python code. To work in Python, you will need to open IDLE because opening Python files directly won't work!

ON A PC

Step1. Click the Windows Start menu.

Step2. Start typing "idle", then select the search result IDLE (Python 3.7 64-bit). Note: Yours might say IDLE (Python 3.7 32-bit) if that's the kind of machine you have.

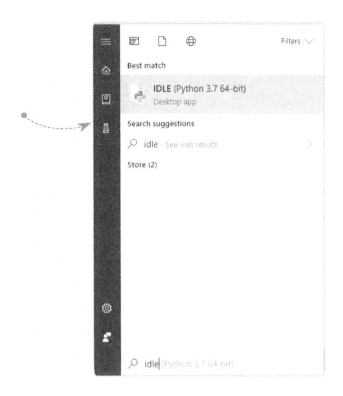

Step3. A window should pop up that looks like this:

Step4. Nice! You opened IDLE on Windows and are now ready to start writing some codes in Python!

ON A MAC

Step1. Navigate to GO > APPLICATIONS.

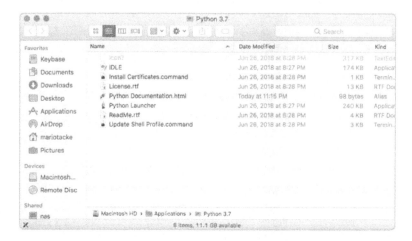

Step2. Find the Python 3.7 folder and open it.

Step3. Double-click on the IDLE icon.

Step4. A window should pop up that looks like this:

```
Python 3.7.0 (v3.7.0:1bf9cc5093, Jun 26 2018, 23:26:24)
[Clang 6.0 (clang-600.0.57)] on darwin
Type "copyright", "credits" or "license()" for more information.
>>>
```

Step5. Congratulations! You opened IDLE on a Mac and are now ready to start writing some code in Python!

Saying hi to python!

Now that you've installed Python and IDLE on your computer, let's say hi! Open up IDLE on your computer whenever you open up the IDLE program on your computer, you will always be brought to the shell first. The shell is the interactive window that allows you to write

Python code within it and then see the results of your code right away. You'll know when you're in the shell because it will say Python 3.7.0 Shell in the title bar of the window.

In your shell, go ahead and type the following code:

print ("Hi Python!")

Now, hit the ENTER key. Do you see something like this?

```
Python 3.7.0 Shell
File  Edit  Shell  Debug  Options  Window  Help
Python 3.7.0 (v3.7.0:1bf9cc5093, Jun 27 2018, 04:59:51) [MSC v.1914 64 bit (AMD6
4)] on win32
Type "copyright", "credits" or "license()" for more information.
>>> print("Hi Python!")
Hi Python!
>>>
```

Great job! You're about to learn some awesome things.

Saving your work

When we go more and deeper into learning python, our programs will probably be a little longer than the ones we write in the beginning. Wouldn't it be useful if we could save our progress so we don't have to re-type all the code we write? Of course it would! This is where saving your work comes in handy.

Even though it's a short program, let's save our Python greeting to its own file so you can see how easy it is to save your work.

First, let's create a new file:

Step1.On the **MENU** bar in your shell, click the **FILE** tab to open its context menu, which is a list of actions that you can perform.

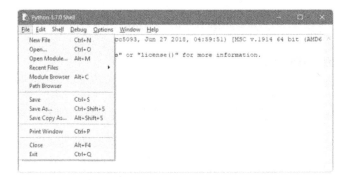

Step2. Click NEW FILE.

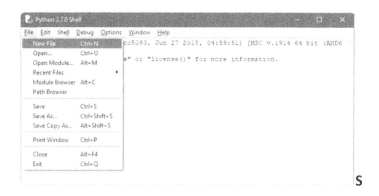

tep3. A new window should pop up, like this:

Step4. Type in your greeting, using Python code: **print ("Hi Python!")**

We have to put our greeting into this piece of Python code so that the computer knows to "write" this message for us onto the screen.

Great! Now you have your code in a file that we can save. This is important, because the first code we wrote was in the shell, which means it won't be saved once you close the window. Writing code directly in the shell is just a quicker way to run Python code and see the results right away. Always create a new file and save it to keep track of your work and save your progress!

Now that we have created a file with our greeting code, let's save it. You can save your program in IDLE by following these next steps.

Step5. On the **MENU** bar of your shell, click the **FILE** tab to open its context menu.

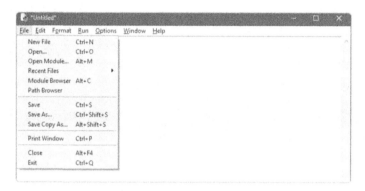

Step6. Click **SAVE**.

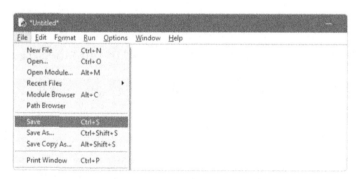

Step7. The next window will ask you to name your file. Go ahead and give it a name. I'll call mine "greeting."

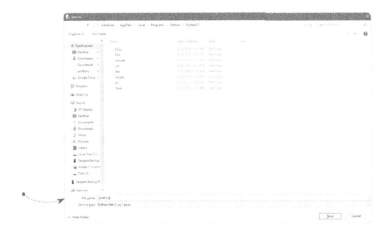

Step8. Make sure to save your Python program in a place that you won't forget! If you don't choose another place, new files are usually saved in the same folder as the Python download, so go ahead and change the "Save In" place to a better spot. I created a folder called **COOL PYTHON** in my **DOCUMENTS** directory, so that's where I'll save my programs.

Step9. Click **SAVE**. That's it! Another step forward for you!

Running a program

This is the best part—seeing your code in action! After you write some code, save it, and are ready to see it run, follow these steps to run your code (skip to step 4 if you already have your program open in its own window).

Step1.On the MENU bar in your shell, click the FILE tab to open the context menu.

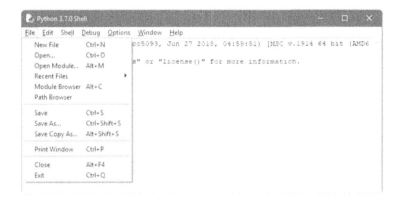

Step2.Click OPEN.

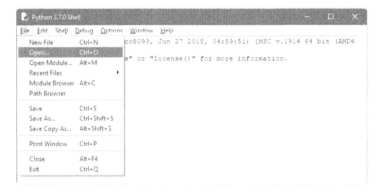

Step3. A window will pop up asking you to pick the file you want to open. Go ahead and find your greeting program and select it. Click OPEN.

Step4. Your program should open in its own window.

Step5. Press the F5 key. That's it! Your code should now execute, meaning the computer will carry out the task you asked it to do in code. You told it to print something, and it did! You should see your greeting in the shell.

```
Python 3.7.0 Shell                                        -  □  x
File Edit Shell Debug Options Window Help
Python 3.7.0 (v3.7.0:1bf9cc5093, Jun 27 2018, 04:59:51) [MSC v.1914 64 bit (AMD6
4)] on win32
Type "copyright", "credits" or "license()" for more information.
>>>
======== RESTART: C:\Users\Adrienne\Documents\Cool Python\greeting.py ========
Hi Python!
>>> |
```

✓ Troubleshooting Tip: Is the F5 key not working for you? Some computers require you to press the Fn button along with the F5 button. Go ahead, try that instead!

Chapter 5

Python Data Types

In this chapter, we'll get right into understanding how Python works and we'll start by looking at the data types available in Python.

A data type is a particular kind of data item usually defined by the values it can take or the operations that can be performed on it. What this is saying essentially is that there are different types of data. You're most likely familiar with things like numbers, letters, and dates. All of these are types of data or data types. Python has its own data types, some of which are similar to the data types you're already familiar with and others, not so much.

Before we delve into the data types available in Python, we'll do a quick check to make sure you understand what data types are. Let's see how well you answer the question below.

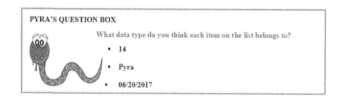

If your answer looks like the list below, great work! You're ready to dive into Python data types.

PYRA'S SUGGESTION

14 – Numbers

Pyra – Letters

06/20/2017 - Date

Numbers

In Python, the number data type consists of numeric values like 1, 17.66 and 109967675412. There are different number types and they're listed below.

int: This data type includes integers like 4, 806, -130 and 1399. Integers are whole numbers. They do not have a fractional part. Integers can be positive or negative numbers.

long: This data type includes long numbers like 44778234567600. Long numbers are numbers that are generally larger than those used in everyday math.

float: This data type includes floating point numbers like 72.17, 33.6 and 1.00814. Floating point numbers have a fractional part which is not fixed. This means that there can be any number of digits before and after the decimal point.

complex: This data type includes complex numbers like x + zn or 4 + 1/2x. Complex numbers have a real and imaginary part.

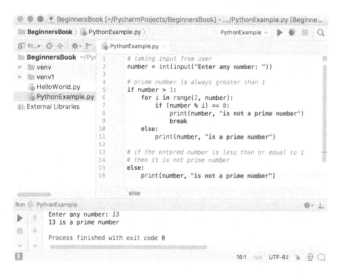

Sequences

Python data types that exist in a sequence are known as sequences. There are different types of sequences and they are described below.

Strings: In Python, a string is a contiguous set of characters like "Romeo" or "Juliet". What we described as letters earlier is referred to as strings. A string is made up of characters. For example, the string

"Romeo" has 5 characters. Can you tell Pyre what they are? That's exactly right! The characters in the string "Romeo" are r, o, m, e and o.

Strings in Python are placed within quotation marks. They can be single quotation marks or double quotation marks like this: 'Romeo' or "Romeo". Whenever Python sees anything in quotation marks, it knows that's a string.

Lists: In Python, a list contains items which are separated by commas and enclosed in square brackets like this: ['Mary', 'Eric' 'and', 'Shawn']. Lists are interesting because they can contain items which are of different data types like this: [4, 'Mary', 'Angela', 200]. It is important to remember that lists must be contained within square brackets. You can change the size of a list or the items inside a list after it has been created. Whenever Python sees any list of items separated by commas and enclosed in square brackets, it knows that's a list.

```
tuple_examples.py
1   single_item_tuple = ("Hello")
2
3   print(type(single_item_tuple))
4
5   single_item_tuple = (10)
6
7   print(type(single_item_tuple))
8
```

Run: tuple_examples
/Users/pankaj/Documents/PycharmProject
<class 'str'>
<class 'int'>

Process finished with exit code 0

195

Tuples: In Python, a tuple is a sequence data type which contains items separated by commas and enclosed in parenthesis like this: ('Spiderman', ironman' 'and' 'superman'). Tuples are similar to lists because they contain items separated by commas but they are different from lists because their items are enclosed in parenthesis and not square brackets. Tuples cannot be changed after they are created. Tuples can exist without their enclosing parenthesis like a, b, c but an empty tuple must have the enclosing parenthesis like this (). A tuple with a single item must have a trailing comma like (p,). Whenever Python sees a list of items separated by commas and enclosed in parenthesis, it knows that's a tuple.

Byte: In Python, a byte is a sequence of integers in the range of 0 – 255. Bytes are immutable which means that they can't be changed after they are created.

Bytearray: A bytearray data type is similar to a byte data type but is mutable. This means that objects of this data type can be altered/changed after they are created.

Sequence items are accessed through their index number. Indices start from zero (0) and increases upwards e.g. 0, 1, 2, 3 etc. So, if you had a list named "fruit_list" containing the items ['oranges', 'strawberries', 'apples', 'bananas'], you can access each item in the list like this.

fruit_list[0] = oranges

fruit_list[1] = strawberries

fruit_list[2] = apples

fruit_list[3] = bananas

For example, to print out "apples" from the list above, the print statement will be written like this.

print(fruit_list[2])

```
pytestpackage
1  fruit_list = ['oranges', 'strawberries', 'apples', 'bananas']
2
3  print(fruit_list[2])
4
5
6
7
8
```

```
Console
<terminated> __init__.py [C:\Users\
apples
```

Let's try the same thing for a string.

```
pytestpackage
1  name = 'Barney'
2
3  print(name[3])
4
5
```

```
Console
<terminated> __init__.py [C:\Users\
n
```

Sets

Sets in Python are just like sets in Math. They are similar to lists and tuples but unlike lists and tuples, they cannot have multiple occurrences of the same element or item. This means that you can't have a set where one item is repeated more than once like ('a', 'b', 'c', 'a'). There are two types of sets in Python.

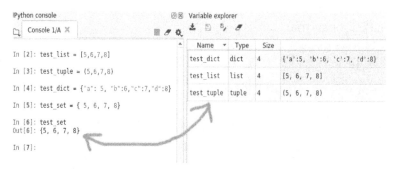

Sets: A set is an unordered collection of unique items. The items inside a set cannot be changed after they've been created but the set itself can be changed. For example, you can append more items to an existing set. Here's what we mean. If we have a set named states which contains the items Washington, New York and Pennsylvania, we can't change New York to anything else but we can append another state e.g. Texas to the states set so the set now contains the items Washington, New York, Pennsylvania and Texas.

A set is enclosed in parenthesis just like tuples but they are different from tuples because they are mutable. Do you remember what being mutable means? It means that a set can be altered or changed after it has been created whereas a tuple cannot. Sets can't contain multiple occurrences of the same element, unlike tuples where the same element can be repeated. Another difference between a set and a tuple is that you can't look up the items in a set by index (we'll explain indices later) whereas you can do so for tuples.

Frozen sets: A frozen set is an immutable set. This is essentially a set which cannot be changed after it is created.

Mappings

A mapping data type contains objects which map fixed values to arbitrary objects. Mappings are mutable which means that they can be altered or changed after they have been created. As at the time of writing this book, we only have one standard mapping data type in Python and that is the dictionary data type or dict.

Dictionary: In Python, a dictionary is an unordered list of "key – value" pairs. Dictionaries are similar to lists but they are enclosed in curly braces {} rather than square brackets and contain items which are pairs of keys and their corresponding values. For example, the dictionary below contains three keys. The first key is named FirstKey and has a value of 200. The second key is named SecondKey and has a value of "Mary". The third key is named ThirdKey and has a value of 4. Dictionary keys are separated from their corresponding values with a colon as seen in the dictionary below.

mydictionary = {'FirstKey': 200, 'SecondKey': "Mary", 'ThirdKey': 4}

Boolean

The Boolean data type holds only two types of data – True or False. In arithmetic contexts, Boolean values behave like the integer values 0 and 1.

```
Python 3.6.0 (v3.6.0:41df79263a11, Dec 23 2016, 07:18:10) [MSC v.1900 32 bit (
Intel)] on win32
Type "copyright", "credits" or "license()" for more information.
>>> bool(1)
True
>>> bool(0)
False
>>> bool()
False
>>> bool(
     bool(x) -> bool
```

Mutable vs Immutable data types

Data types in Python are distinguished based on whether it is possible to alter/change objects of that type after they have been created. If yes, that data type is said to be mutable. If not, that data type is said to be immutable. The table below shows the data types we've already learned about distinguished into mutable or immutable data types.

MUTABLE DATA TYPES	IMMUTABLE DATA TYPES
list	int
set	float
dict	long
byte array	complex
	str
	byte
	tuple
	frozen set

Chapter exercises

What data type do you think 'A' in the expression below is?

A = ['sunshine', 'rain', 'thunderstorm']

PYRA'S SUGGESTION
A string is composed of characters. Count the number of characters you can see in the string and write the number here ----------.

How many characters are in the string "universe"?

'A' in the expression below is a string in Python. True or False?

A = Romeo.

PYRA'S SUGGESTION
Strings in Python are written a certain way. Is Romeo written the way strings in Python should be written? If yes, write 'True'. If no, write 'False' here ----------.

What data type is 'A' in the expression below?

A = ("Tomorrow", 500, "lights", "average", "Tomorrow")

PYRA'S SUGGESTION
Whenever Python sees a list of items separated by commas and enclosed within parenthesis, it knows that's a ----------.

What data type in Python will be best to store the data below?

Aiden: 'Male'

Sarah: 'Female'

Monica: 'Female'

202

Shawn: 'Male'

Chapter 6

Variables and Operators

So now that we've got Python installed and an IDE set up, we're ready to begin learning Python for real. The following will focus on introducing core Python concepts like variables, operators, and the various types of data you can manipulate with Python. For now, let's concentrate on understanding variables and operators.

Variables

When you hear the word "variable," what do you think of? There's a good chance you might think back to algebra class and recall that a variable was often a letter that represents some number. In other words, it was one item that contained a representation of another item. Generally, in Python and programming, that's what variables are. They are just representations of data stored in a form that is easy to access and manipulate. Let's try creating some variables now.

X = 30

That's a very common usage of a variable. Just like you'd see in math class, "X" represents the numerical value 30. However, variables can also store other types of data, like text.

Weather = "cloudy"

Here, we're asserting that the "weather" variable has the word "cloudy" stored in it. When we use the "equals" sign in Python, unlike in math, we aren't saying that the two values are equal. Rather, we're "assigning" or storing a value in a variable that will contain the representation of that value. We'll talk more about this when we cover operators, but for now, just know that in Python (and in programming languages generally); the equals sign is used differently to the mathematical equals sign.

As far as naming our variables goes, the variable can basically be called anything if they adhere to a few rules:

- Contains only letters, numbers, or underscores
- First character is not a number
- Variable name is not one of the reserved keywords

Uppercase and lowercase letters are fine, as are any amount of numbers or underscores. Although the first character in the variable name cannot be a number. There are also a few words (like "input," "print," and "while") that cannot be used as variable names because Python uses these words for specific commands. One last important thing to remember is that variable names are case sensitive, so "varName" is a different variable than "varname."

While variables can be named pretty much anything, in practice, you'll want to follow some guidelines when creating variable names. In the past, there were two commonly accepted ways of formatting variable names: camel case and underscoring. Camel case refers to the practice of joining together compound words with upper case letters. (Ex.

variableName, thisIsCamelCase.) Meanwhile, underscoring is just adding underscores between compound variable names, like this: underscore_name, variable_name.

While this was true in older versions of the Python style guide, the preferred variable style is now the use of underscores.

Beyond that, try to name variables things that make sense. Avoid confusing variable names (ex. Cat = "dog") in favor of variable names that make intuitive sense (animal = "dog").

Operators

Let's talk about operators. Operators are symbols that perform functions, and they are used to manipulate data in different ways.

We've already touched on one operator, the assignment operator, which is represented by an equals sign. As mentioned before, the "=" sign in Python has a different meaning to its use in math; here it means that we are assigning the value on the right side of the operator to the variable found on the other side. Let's try using the = operator and assigning some values to some variables.

R = 12

S = 9

T = S

Let's now print out the values of these variables.

print(R)

print(S)

print(T)

Notice that the output of the program is 12, 9, and 9. This is because we declared that R stores the value 12, S stores the value 9, and T stores the same value as S.

Now let's look at some of the other operators to be found in Python. The operators that are found in Python include the addition operator, the subtraction operator, the multiplication operator, the division operator, the floor division operator, the modulus operator, and the exponent operator.

The addition operator: +

The addition operator let's you adds two values together.

Ex. If R = 2 and S = 3, then R + S = 5

The subtraction operator: -

The subtraction operator let's you subtracts the second value from the first.

Ex. If R = 4 and S = 3, then R - S = 1

The multiplication operator: *

The multiplication operator let's you multiplies two values.

Ex. If R = 3 and S = 2, then R * S = 6

The division operator: /

The division operator let's you divides the second value into the first.

Ex. If R = 9 and S = 3, then R / S = 3

The floor division operator: //

The floor division operator divides and then rounds down to the nearest whole number.

Ex. If R = 7 and S = 2, then R // S = 3

The Modulus Operator: %

The Modulus operator produces the remainder of a division operation.

Ex. If R = 7 and S = 2, then R % S = 1

The Exponent Operator: **

The Exponent operator raises the first value to the power of the second value.

Ex. If R = 9 and S = 2, R**S = 81

It's highly advised that you play around with these operators and try writing programs that they can use to practice their application.

Combining Operators

The assignment operator can be combined with other operators like addition, subtraction, and multiplication operators. This makes it easier to carry out operations instead of following multiple steps. To be clearer, here's an example:

Instead of having to write:

R = R * 2

We could just write:

R *= 2

Try experimenting with the other combined operators to see how easy they make updating values.

Chapter 7

Python Strings

Python uses built-in strings assigned to variables. Strings are created by enclosing Python statements in quotes, either single (') quotes or double (") quotes. Creating a string in Python is as easy as creating variables and assigning values.

Assign a String to a Variable

Assigning strings to variables is accomplished by creating a variable, followed by an equal sign and then the string.

x="Hi!"

print (x)

A string can span multiple lines with each line separated by a backslash (\) at the end. String literals can use three double quotes or three single quotes to represent multiple lines of text.

```
str = '####$Hello World'

str_strip = str.lstrip()
print(str_strip)
>>> $Hello World
```

Strings are immutable. That is, once you create strings in Python, you can't change them. Therefore, you have to create new strings to represent computed values. For example, ('Hello' + 'World') have two strings, 'Hello' and 'World', which are used to build a new string 'HelloWorld'.

Accessing Characters in a String

The characters in a string are accessed with the standard [] syntax just like in arrays. Python uses zero indexing to initialize the string. If the string index is out of bounds, an error is generated. Python stops executions if it can't tell what to do, in which case it sends an error message.

To extract characters from the string, enter the string name followed by the index number. For example, to retrieve character 'e' from string 'hello', you write hello [1]. The len (string) function returns the string length.

The [] syntax and len () function works in any sequence in strings or lists. Python uses the '+' operator to concatenate two strings.

Example:

a="Hello"

print a [3]

print len (a)

print a + 'there'

// Output

l

5

Hello there

In some cases, the '+' operator doesn't convert numbers into string type. To do so, use the str () function that converts values to string form so as to combine them with other strings.

Example:

pi=3.14

confirm= 'the value of pi is' + str (pi)

// Output

yes

String Slicing

The slice syntax is a great way to return sub-parts of a string sequence. If you want to return a range of characters, you can use the slice syntax. This allows you to specify the start index and the end index separated by a colon.

To return part of a string in 'Hello World', write:

x='Hello'

Print (x [1:4]

//output

'ell'

In this case, the characters start at index 1 and extend to others characters but don't include the index 4.

```
Hello
0  1  2  3  4
-5 -4 -3 -2 -1
```

x[1:] will return 'ello' – it omits the index defaults at the end (or beginning for x[:4]) of the string.

x[:] will return 'Hello' – since no string index is specified, the code returns the whole string (this is commonly used when you want to copy the entire string or list).

x[2:100] will return 'llo'. If you're working with a big index (in this case 100), it will be truncated down to a string length.

Negative Indexing

You can use negative indexing to write slice syntax from the end of the string. The x[-1] is the last char 'o' and so on.

x[-1] returns 'o' – last character

x[-4] returns 'e' – the fourth character from the end.

x[:-3] returns 'He' – represents characters from the start of the string but doesn't include the last 3 characters.

x[-3:] returns 'llo' – represents characters starting with the third character from the end of the string and extends up to the end of the string.

Note: Python doesn't have any separate scalar 'char' type. If you have a string x[10], Python will return string_length-1 characters. The operators ==, <=, or >= all works the same way. That is, for any index n, the x[:n] +x[n:]==x. This also applies to the negative indexing, -n. The x[:n] and x[n:] partition a Python string into two, thus conserving all the characters.

String Methods

Python has built-in functions or methods that work well with strings. The string method runs 'on' an object. If a created variable is a string, then the lower () or upper() functions run on the string object and return the results. The concept of running methods on objects is why Python is considered an object oriented programming language.

Some of these string methods include:

- Strip() which is used to eliminate the white spaces from the beginning or the end of a string.
- Lower() and upper () methods returns the string in lower case and upper case respectively.
- Startswith(other) and endswith(other) methods measure the start and end of the string.
- Isalpha(), isspace(), and isdigit() are used to test whether the string characters belong to a certain class character.
- Find(other) is used to search for a particular string within the created variable and return the first index where it begins or a -1 if it's found.
- Join(list) is used to join together elements in a given list using the string as the delimiter. For example, join('xxx', 'yyy', 'zzz') -> ['xxx', 'yyy', 'zzz'].
- Split('delim') returns substring list separated by a given delimiter. Delimiter in this case acts as text and not a regular expression that is, 'xxx,yyy,zzz.split('.') –> ['xxx', 'yyy', 'zzz']. The split() with no arguments splits characters with white spaces.
- Replace('old', 'new') returns a string where the old string characters are replaced with new characters.
- Format() is used to format specified values within a string.

- Count() returns the number of times a certain character occurs in the string.

Example 1:

x=Hello World!

Print (x.lower())

This code returns the string in lowercase letters.

Example 2:

x=Hello World!

Print (x.replace('H', 'M'))

When you run the code, the 'Hello' string will be replaced with 'Mello'.

Check String

Check string is used to find out whether a certain character is present in a string. It uses the keyword in and not in to check.

Example:

txt= "Welcome to Python programming for advanced users"

x="ing" in txt

print(x)

```
s = 'Python is Good!'
print(s.title())                    ← Python string title() function

s = 'PYTHON IS GOOD'                  Apostrophes are treated as word
print(s.title())                      boundary, causing unexpected output

s = "Let's go to Party"
print(s.title())

import re
```
Custom Function to convert string to title cased
```
def titlecase(s):
    return re.sub(r"[A-Za-z]+('[A-Za-z]+)?",
                  lambda mo:
                      mo.group(0)[0].upper() +
                      mo.group(0)[1:].lower(), s)


s = "Let's go to Party"
print(titlecase(s))
print(titlecase('Python is Good!'))
print(titlecase('PYTHON IS GOOD'))
```

To check if the phrase "ing" is not in the text:

txt= "Welcome to Python programming for advanced users"

x="ing" not in txt

print(x)

Special String Operators

Operator	Description	Example
+	Concatenation - Adds values on either side of the operator	a + b will give HelloPython
*	Repetition - Creates new strings, concatenating multiple copies of the same string	a*2 will give HelloHello
[]	Slice - Gives the character from the given index	a[1] will give e
[:]	Range Slice - Gives the characters from the given range	a[1:4] will give ell
in	Membership - Returns true if a character exists in the given string	H in a will give 1
not in	Membership - Returns true if a character does not exist in the given string	M not in a will give 1
r/R	Raw String - Suppresses actual meaning of Escape characters. The syntax for raw strings is exactly the same as for normal strings with the exception of the raw string operator, the letter "r," which precedes the quotation marks. The "r" can be lowercase (r) or uppercase (R) and must be placed immediately preceding the first quote mark.	print r'\n' prints \n and print R'\n' prints \n

Strings can be manipulated using one of the following operators.

String Formatting Operator (%)

Python consists of the string formatting operator %. The % operator is a unique string feature that uses functions from the C language family's printf() function. Python accepts a printf-type string format with %d for integer values, %s for string, and %f for floating point numbers on the left and matching values on the right in a tuple. A tuple consists of values grouped within parentheses and separated by commas.

Example:

Print ("My name is %s and my weight is %d kg!" %('Faith', 50))

When the above code is executed, it will display:

My name is Faith and my weight is 50kg!

The list below is a set of samples that can be used together with the % operator.

Other supported samples include:

Unicode String

Normal Python strings are stored using the 8-bit ASCII code. Unicode strings are stored using the 16-bit Unicode. This enables the string to accommodate a varied set of characters.

Chapter Summary

In this chapter, you learned:

- How to create strings in python
- How to access characters in a string

- How to use slicing feature to return sub-parts of a string
- How to apply various methods to manipulate strings like isalpha(), isspace(), isdigit(), strip(), and find() among other methods.
- How to format strings using the % operator.

Chapter 8

Loops

A loop is a piece of code that is repeated until certain conditions are met.

An example of a loop is this:

Wake up

Eat

Sleep

Repeat

A lot of us people carry out this loop daily. In other words, a loop is a circle that goes on and on.

Another example of a loop is this.

Wake up

Dress up

Go to school

Go back home

Sleep

Except on Saturday and Sunday

Pseudocode

When you wish to write a program, pseudocode is what you first write down. It is the expression of your code in standard English.

It allows you to think about how you want to solve the problem without first worrying about the details of the code.

Example:

Pseudocode for a game:

Introduction

\# get a random number

\# create a loop

\# ask for programmer input

\# tell user result

\# ask user to play again

\# congratulate user

For another game

\# design interface

\# create ball

\# create bounce pads

\# make ball move

\# create scoring system

\# create winning criteria.

Now under each of these sections, the code needed for the computer to carry out these actions is written.

Pseudocode helps you to easily correct mistakes in your code as you can easily find where an error or a glitch is coming from. It also helps your code to be orderly and neat and also make it easy for other programmers to understand your code.

When you use pseudocode inside your text editor, you need to make it invisible to the computer or python interpreter. For this, you need the hash sign.

Hash Sign and the triple comma

The hash sign and the triple comma are used to make things that you write in your text editor invisible to your python interpreter.

Example

\>>> #print ('I love shopping')

\>>> print ("I love volley ball")

R: the first print is not obeyed because it is invisible to the computer. The most critical uses of this is writing pseudo code.

The (,,,) triple comma is used to make large blocks of code invisible to the python interpreter.

Example

>>> ,,,

\>>> #print ('I love shopping')

\>>> print ("I love volley ball")

>>> print ('I will talk')

>>> print ('I will run')

>>> ,,,

>>> print ('football')

R: football

This is because the parts of code in between the triple commas above and below are invisible to the computer.

While Loops

The while loop consists of a 'while' statement and a piece of code that is to run if the while statement is true.

The while statement is often a Boolean. The piece of code that follows the while statement is commonly referred to as the body of the loop.

The bit of code that comes after the while statement is indented. This is commonly done with 4 spaces rather than a tab.

When you type the while statement, however, IDLE automatically indents for you.

When you are finished entering the statement(s) that make up the body of the loop, you can press Backspace (Windows) or the Delete (Mac) key to move the indenting level back four spaces.

Examples:

As long as the Boolean expression in the while statement evaluates to True, the comments in the body of the loop are repeated.

If the Boolean definition evaluates to False, the body of the loop is skipped, and execution continues with the first statement after the shape of the loop.

Example:

In the following code, we'll ask the user to type the letter a, and we'll keep asking until the user types an a:

```
>>> looping = True
>>> while looping == True: answer = input("Please type the letter 'a': ")
>>> if answer == 'a':
>>> looping = False # we're done
>>> else:
>>>print("Come on, type an 'a'!)"
```

```
>>>print("Thanks for typing an 'a'")
```

Before the loop starts, we set a Boolean variable named looping to True. The Boolean expression in this while statement compares the Boolean to the value True. We also could also have written it as follows:

looping = True

while looping:

This would work the same way because comparing a Boolean to True is the same as just the value of the Boolean itself.

At the end of the loop, the Python interpreter automatically goes back to the while statement at the top of the loop.

As long as the variable that is looping has a value of True, the code in the body of the loop will be copied.

When we want to end the loop, something (a piece of code) in the body of the loop must make the loop false.

In this loop, when the user types the letter a, we set looping to False.

When this piece of code that falsifies the whole loop is reached, the while statement of the loop is rendered false, and we then exit the loop.

For the above reason, the Boolean expression in the while statement is also called the exit condition — the condition under which you can exit the loop.

If we don't have any code that changes the exit condition, we would have on our hands an infinite loop (a loop that keeps running without stopping)

Trying Loops in a Real Program

The way the program works is this:

The program will ask the programmer for a number.

The program will then add all the numbers below the picked number to the chosen number.

That is when the programmer enters 9; then the computer will add 1, 2, 3, 4, 5, 6, 7, and 8 to 9 and then give an answer.

#first loop program

x = input('Enter a target number: ')

x = int(target)

y = 0

your_number = 1

while your_number<= target:

add in the next value

```
y = y + your_number #add in the next number
your_number = your_number + 1
print('your answer to', x, 'is:', y)
```

First, we get a number from the programmer and get it converted to an integer.

We then set y to 0; y is to hold the total of all the numbers.

We also set the your_number variable to 1. The your_number variable will be used to add the numbers from 1 to the number that the programmer entered.

What followed was that they wrote our while statement.

We specified that the loop should keep going until the your_number is higher than the number in x. When this happens, the while statement becomes False, and the loop is exited.

Every time through the loop, we add the value of your_number to x.

Eventually, we add one to what is in your_number to get to the next number.

This piece of code is the key to exiting the loop because the code will stop once the while statement (while your_number<= target) is no longer true.

When you run the program, for example, with 8.

You will get

R: your answer to', x, 'is:', y)

Increment and Decrement

The program we you just wrote,

your_number = your_number + 1

It is a piece of code that adds your_number to 1 and puts in the result into the variable your_number.

This method of increasing the value of a variable is called an Increment.

For the above program, we had an increment by 1, but an increment can be by any number.

Our above example is a way of incrementing a variable. There is another way to do the same thing.

your_number + =1

In this method, you use the plus and the equals operators, and it gives you the exact same thing as this your_number = your_number + 1.

The opposite of an increment is a decrement.

A decrement is when a variable subtracts from itself.

Example

your_number = your_number - 1

or

your_number -= 1

Built-in Packages

Python language has some keywords (if, elif, else, while, def, and a few more) and built-in functions (int, str, input, and so on).

Apart from these, Python also has some prewritten packages of code that are built-in and are available to programmers.

These packages were installed on your computer when you installed Python.

They are called the Python Standard Library.

There are also "external packages" written by older and more experienced programmers. They make their codes available to other programmers.

External packages are downloaded separately from the internet.

Examples of external packages are Loguru, Monkeytype, Pyright, PyGame, mp.py, etc.

These external packages help you to do different things. PyGame, for example, helps you to build games

When you want to use a build in the package, you have to tell python by using 'import'

Example

import <packageName>

Generating Random Numbers

Random package is an in built package that is used to create random numbers.

It contains several functions that allow it to generate random numbers.

Since it is a built-in package, you already have it on your computer.

To import random package, type into your text editor:

import random

When you write a program that uses an import statement, you typically place any import statement(s) at the top of your code. If you want to see the documentation of all the functions that are available in this package, you can call the built-in help function and pass in the name of the package, like this:

help(random)

If you do this, you will get screens and screens worth of documentation. In you are truly interested in the details of all the functions, feel free to read through this documentation. There are a large number of functions that you can call in the random package. For now, we are interested in one specific function named randrange.

The purpose of randrange is to generate a random integer number within a given range. randrange is interesting because the range itself can be specified in a number of different ways, with different numbers of arguments. Using the most straightforward form, we'll call the randrange function specifying the range as two integers. Here is the way we call it:

random.randrange(<lowValue>, <upToButNotIncludingHighValue>)

You start by specifying the name of the package—in this case, the word random. After the package name, you type a period (generally read as "dot"). After the dot, you specify the function you want to call; in this case, you type randrange to say that you want to use that specific function. In the preceding line, randrange expects to be called with two arguments: a low-end value and a high-end value. The low-end value is included in the range, but the high-end value is not included in the range. The way that we say this is "up to but not including" the high-end value. (We'll see this "up to but not including" concept many times in Python.)

The function returns an integer within the specified range. The most typical way to use randrange is in an assignment statement, where you save the returned value in a variable, like this:

<resultVariable> = random.randrange(<lowValue>, <upToButNotIncludingHighValue>)

Here are some examples:

```
#random between 1 and 10
aRandomNumber = random.randrange(1, 11)
#random between 1 and 52, to pick a card number from a deck
anotherRandomNumber = random.randrange(1, 53)
```

The critical thing to remember (which may seem very odd) is that the second argument needs to be one more than the top end of your intended range. That's because the number you specify here is not included in the range.

As an alternative syntax, you can call randrange with only a single argument: the "up to but not including" high end. If you make this call with only the one argument, randrange assumes that the low end of your range is zero:

```
#random between 0 and 8
myRandomNumber = random.randrange(9)   # same as random.randrange(0, 8)
```

Chapter 9

For Loop

We will discuss the for loop. Just like a while loop, the for loop also repeatedly executes a set of code while the condition holds true. Once the condition becomes false, it will come out of the loop. Some basic requirements of a for loop are:

It must refer to a list or a range

It ends with a (:) colon

The code which has to be executed should be indented by one tab space

---

Example3:

First Example

for letter in 'Python':

  print 'Current Letter :', letter

Output:

Current Letter : P

Current Letter : y

Current Letter : t

Current Letter : h

Current Letter : o

Current Letter : n

Second Example

```
fruits = ['apple', 'banana','mango'];
for fruit in fruits:
    print 'Current fruit :', fruit
print "Good bye!"
```

Output:

Current fruit : apple

Current fruit : banana

Current fruit : mango

Good bye!

Measure some strings

```
words = ['cat', 'apple', 'defenestrate']
for w in words:
    print w, len(w)
```

Output:

```
cat 3

window 6

defenestrate 12
```

Nested loops

A loop with in a loop, or loops with in a loop are said to be the nested loops. The nested loops can be of both, a for loop or a while loop.

The syntax for a nested loop is as follows:

    for condition1:

for condition2:

code_to_execute2

code_to_execute1

while condition1:

while condition2:

code_to_execute2

code_to_execute1

Nested for loop

Example4:

w =['a','b','c'];

x =['d','e','f'];

y =['g','h','i'];

z =[i,j,k];

c =1;

for item in w:

print m

for element in item:

print element

m=m+1

Output:

1 ; a; b; c; 2; d; e; f; 3; g; h; i

Nested While loop

Example5:

```
x =1;
y=10;
z=20;
while x<y:
print 'x= ',x;
print 'x is less than y';
x=x+5;
while y<z:
print 'y= ',y;
print 'y is greater than x but less than z';
y=y+4;
```

Output:

x = 1

x is less than y

y = 10

y is greater than x but less than z

y = 14

y is greater than x but less than z

y = 18

> y is greater than x but less than z
>
> x = 6
>
> x is less than y
>
> x = 11
>
> x is less than y
>
> x = 16
>
> x is less than y
>
> x = 21
>
> x is less than y

Control Statements

To execute a loop in a normal and smooth flow we use the control statements. Let us go through different types of control statements that can be used in loops along with the examples.

In a programming life cycle, sometimes you may face a scenario where you want to jump out of a certain loop once a specified condition holds true.

Example6:

```
j = 0
for i in range(5):
    j = j + 2
    print ('i= ', i, ', j = ', j)
    if j == 6:
        break;
```

Output:

i = 0 , j = 2

i = 1 , j = 4

i = 2 , j = 6

If we had not used the break statement, then the loop would have run further until i's value turned 4 since the range was mentioned 5. But with the break statement, the loop ends prematurely when i reach the value 2. This is due to the condition before the break statement, which became true when j reached 6.

Example7:

```
x=1
while x<11:
if(x%2==0):
print 'x is even ',x;
else:
print 'x is odd',x;
x=x+1
if(x==5):
break;
print 'I will not go further';
```

Output:

x is odd 1

x is even 2

x is odd 3

x is even 4

I will not go further

Another useful control statement for the loops is the continue keyword. When you use continue, remaining part of the code of the loop gets skipped for that particular iteration only.

Example8:

j = 0

for i in range(5):

j = j + 2;

print ('\ni= ', i, ', j = ', j);

if j == 6:

continue;

print ('I will be skipped over if j=6');

Output:

i = 0 , j = 2

I will be skipped over if j=6

i = 1 , j = 4

I will be skipped over if j=6

i = 2 , j = 6

```
i = 3 , j = 8
I will be skipped over if j=6
i = 4 , j = 10
I will be skipped over if j=6
```

Example9:

```
x = 10;
while x:
x=x – 1;
ifx%2!=0:
continue;
print(x,'is even and less than 10');
Output:
8 is even and less than 10
6 is even and less than 10
4 is even and less than 10
```

```
2 is even and less than 10

0 is even and less than 10
```

Pass

The pass statement is used when you have a method or statement that you want to keep but not take any action. The pass statement is a null operation and nothing happens when it executes, this makes it ideal for testing new development as it can be used as a sort of place holder for incomplete sections of code that would otherwise have thrown an error.

Example10:

```
for letter in 'Python':
  if letter == 'h':
    pass
    print 'This is pass block'
  print 'Current Letter :', letter
print "Good bye!"
```

```
Output:

Current Letter : P

Current Letter : y

Current Letter : t

This is pass block

Current Letter : h

Current Letter : o

Current Letter : n

Good bye!
```

Arrays

Arrays are one of the most basic data structures used in any programming language. In Python, there is no native data structure for arrays instead lists are used as multidimensional arrays.

In this chapter, you will learn how to work with lists and treat them as arrays. You can also use libraries in Python for handling extensive array operations and numeric arrays. However, we will only be covering some basic array operations provided in Python.

List vs. Array

Before we delve into arrays, let us recap the lists. A group of related items stored together is referred to as a list. You can also store these items in separate variables. A list can basically contain any item, even another list. Thus, a list can have more than one list in it and can have elements of different data types. In comparison to a list, array is a collection of related elements but of unique data type. The elements cannot vary in the data type. Thus a list is considered to be much more flexible than arrays but it can become difficult to deal with this flexibility when a programmer has to work with regular structure.

Any time during the programming lifecycle, you can add more items to the list, delete the items, sort your list and also search through the items to get the desired value. We can simply declare a list by assigning the values to it which are separated by a coma and square brackets i.e. list_Name = [initial values].

Create an array

Before you create an array in Python, you will first have to import the standard array module. Reason being, as mentioned above, Python does not support a native data structure for arrays instead lists are used. You can import the array module by following statement.

    from array import *

Now that you have imported the module, you can declare an array using the following syntax:

array_Name = array (typecode, [values of array])

Here typecode is the type of elements the array will consist of.

Example1:
my_Array = array ('i', [0, 1, 2, 3, 4, 5, 6]);

The typecode 'i' represents the integer type with 2 bytes size. You can find a detailed list of typecodes which are used in arrays to declare the type of the elements.

Basic array operations

Given below are different basic set of operations that you can perform on an array. Various methods are also listed below along with an example for you to understand the concept of array further and to learn the handling of arrays.

Create and print an array

Now let us create a simple array and then print it.

Example2:

```
from array import *

my_array = array ('i', [1, 2, 3, 4, 5]);

for i in my_array:

print(i);

Output:

1 2 3 4 5
```

Access an array

We can access each element of the array using the indexes. The indexes normally start from 0 instead of 1. Thus the first item of the list has an index value of 0, the next is 1 and so on.

Example3:

```
from array import *

my_array = array ('i', [1, 2, 3, 4, 5]);

print my_array[1];

print my_array[3];
```

```
print my_array[0];
Output:
2 4 1
```

Append() method

To add a new element to an already existing array, we can use the append method.

```
Example4:

from array import *
my_array = array ('i', [1, 2, 3, 4, 5]);
my_array.append(6);
for i in my_array:
print(i);
Output:
1 2 3 4 5 6
```

Insert value in an array

You can use the insert() method to insert an element to an array giving the index where the element is to be added. In the example below, value 6 is being added at the 5th index

Example5:

from array import *
my_array = array ('i', [1, 2, 3, 4, 5]);
my_array.insert(5, 6);
for i in my_array:
print(i);
Output:
1 2 3 4 5 6

Extend an array

You can extend an array, and add more than one value to it. For this you can simply create an array with the elements you want to add to your original array. Pass this array in the extend() method. Your original array will now have the added elements too.

Example6:

from array import *

my_array = array ('i', [1, 2, 3, 4, 5]);

my_extend_array = array('i', [6, 7,8,9,10]);

my_array.extend(my_extend_array);

for i in my_array:

print(i);

Output:

1 2 3 4 5 6 7 8 9 10

Add element from list into array

To copy an element to your array from a list you can use the fromlist() method.

Example7:

from array import *

my_array = array ('i', [1, 2, 3, 4, 5]);

c = [7, 8, 9];

my_array.fromlist(c);

for i in my_array:

print(i);

Output:

1 2 3 4 5 7 8 9

Delete an element

You can use the remove() method to delete an element from the array.

Example8:

from array import *

my_array = array ('i', [1, 2, 3, 4, 5]);

```
my_array.remove(3);
for i in my_array:
print(i);
Output:
1 2 4 5
```

pop() method

To remove the last element of array, pop() method can be used.

Example9:

from array import *
my_array = array ('i', [1, 2, 3, 4, 5]);
my_array.pop();
for i in my_array:
print(i);
Output:
1 2 3 4

Fetch an element through index

You can fetch any element from an array by mentioning the index of that particular element.

Example10:

from array import *

my_array = array ('i', [1, 2, 3, 4, 5]);

my_array.index(1);

Output:

2

Reverse an array

To reverse the entire order of the array, reverse() method is used. This method will reverse all the elements present in the array, placing the first element at the last index, second element at the second last index and so on.

Example11:

```
from array import *
my_array = array ('i', [1, 2, 3, 4, 5, 6, 7, 8, 9, 10]);
my_array.reverse();
for i in my_array:
print(i);
```
Output:

10 9 8 7 6 5 4 3 2 1

Chapter 10

IF, statement

At this point we have already gone over a lot of the most important components of any programming language. Variable, loops and operations are all crucial for any program and inputs also play an important role a lot of the time.

But there is perhaps nothing that characterizes programming as a whole quite as well as the 'IF, THEN' statement. This is a little sequence of code that basically tests a condition and produces output based on that. The result is an instruction that reads 'if this, do that'.

For instance then, we can allow a user only to progress when they've answered a question correctly, or when they have entered the correct password.

But before we get onto that, there is one more thing you need to know about...

Comparing Variables

We are going to carry on with It and Then in a bit but before we do, there's one more thing to consider: comparing variables.

Sometimes it will be useful to look at one variable and then compare that to another variable. For instance, we might want to compare a string to a stored password if we are asking someone to log in. Alternatively, we might be trying to find out if someone is older or younger than a certain age.

To do this, we have a few symbols and conventions. To ask if something 'equals' something else, we will use the symbol '==' (using '==' compares two variables, whereas one '=' forces them to be the same). This is what will allow us to test certain conditions for our IF, THEN statements. This way we can say 'IF' password is correct, 'THEN' proceed.

For example:

Password = "guest"

Attempt = "guest"

if Attempt == Password:

   print("Password Correct")

This essentially tests the imaginary password attempt against the true password and only says 'correct' when the two strings are the same. Notice that we are not actually using the word 'next' at any point. In some programming languages (such as BASIC) you actually do write 'next' but in most it is implicit. Anything that comes after the colon is next, which is just the same way that loops work! Python is nice and consistent and it is actually a very attractive and simple language to look at when you code with it well...

(That is right – programming languages can be attractive! In fact, there is even such thing as 'code poems'!)

We can also use an input to make this a bit more interactive!

Doing this is very easy:

Password = "guest"

Attempt = input("Please enter password: ")if Attempt == Password:

   print("Password Correct")

Try entering the right password and you should be presented with the correct message – congrats!

There is just one problem at the moment, which is that our user will still be able to get into the program if they get the program wrong! And there is nothing to tell them that they answered incorrectly...

Fortunately, we can fix this with our next statement: 'else'.

As you might already have guessed, 'else' simply tells us what to do if the answer is not correct.

This means we can say:

Password = "guest"

Attempt = input("Please enter password: ")
if Attempt == Password:

   print("Password Correct")

       else:

   print("Password Incorrect!")

Note that the 'else' statement moves back to be in-line with the initial 'if' statement. Try entering wrong passwords on purpose now and the new program will tell you have made a mistake!

Okay, so far so good! But now we have another problem: even though our user is entering the password wrong and being told as much, they are still getting to see whatever code comes next:

Password = "guest"

Attempt = input("Please enter password: ")
if Attempt == Password:

   print("Password Correct")

       else:

   print("Password Incorrect!")

print("Secret information begins here...")

Of course this somewhat negates the very purpose of having a password in the first place!

So now we can use something else we learned earlier – the loop! And better yet, we are going to use while True, break and continue. Told you they had come in handy!

```
Password = "guest"

while True:

    Attempt = input("Please enter password: ")

    if Attempt == Password:

        print("Password Correct")

        break

    else:

        print("Password Incorrect!")

        continue

print("Secret information begins here...")
```

Okay, this is starting to get a little more complex and use multiple concepts at once, so let us go through it!

Basically, we are now starting a loop that will continue until interrupted. Each time that loop repeats itself, it starts by asking for input and waits for the user to try the password. Once it has that information, it tests the attempt to see if it is correct or not. If it is, it breaks the loop and the program continues.

If it is not? Then the loop refreshes and the user has another attempt to enter their password!

We've actually gone on something of a tangent here but you may recall that the title of this was 'Comparing Variables'. What if we do not want to test whether two variables are the same? What if we want to find out if one variable is bigger than another? We can ask if something is 'bigger' using the symbol '>' and ask whether it is smaller using the '<' symbol. This is easy to remember – just look at the small end and the big end of the character!

Adding an equal's sign will make this test inclusive. In other words '>=' means 'equal or bigger than'.

Likewise, we may also test if two strings are different. We do this like so: '!=' which basically means 'not equal to'.

Using that last example, we can turn our password test on its head and achieve the exact same end result:

```
Password = "guest"

while True:

    Attempt = input("Please enter password: ")

    if Attempt != Password:

        print("Password Incorrect!")

        continue

    else:

        print("Password Correct")

        break

print("Secret information begins here...")
```

Of course when you get programming you'll find much more useful ways to use this symbol!

Elif and Or

Else is one more command you need to learn to use If statements properly. Equally important though is 'Elif'. Elif is essentially a portmanteau (two words combined) of the words 'Else' and 'If'.

So what we now have is a statement that gives the following instruction:

'If this is true, do this' (IF)

'If that's not true, but this is, then do this' (ELSE IF – ELIF)

'Or else, do this' (ELSE)

So what might this look like? Here is a little example of some code that talks to you differently dependent on your gender. You might find that this also contains another new word you are not familiar with...

Gender = input("Are you male or female? ")

if Gender == "male" or Gender == "Male":

   print("Hello sir!")

elif Gender == "female" or Gender == "Female":

   print("Hello ma'am!")

else:

   print("What is one of those?")

The new word in question is of course 'or'. Let us see how all this works...

Basically, our program is asking you to tell it if you are male or female. If you say male, it calls you sir. If you don't say male but you do say female, then it says 'hello ma'am'.

If you say something else entirely though, then it gets a little confused and asks what you just said.

The 'or' meanwhile, let us perform the same if either one of two statements is true. In this case, we are allowing the program to proceed with either the lower case 'female' or proper case 'Female'. There are other ways to do this but this is a good way to demonstrate the power of 'or'.

If it were not for or, we would be forced to do this:

Gender = input("Are you male or female? ")

if Gender == "male":

   print("Hello sir!")

elif Gender == "Male":

print("Hello sir!")

elif Gender == "female":

   print("Hello ma'am!")

```
elif Gender == "Female":

    print("Hello ma'am!")
else:

   print("What is one of those?")
```

This is another good demonstration of how some code can be more elegant than other code. You might wonder why it matters but when you come to look back over this and you have to sift through thousands of lines, it actually makes all the difference. Moreover, reducing the amount of writing you have to do will save you time and energy – and will also mean the programs you write actually run more quickly!

Chapter Game!

We have talked an awful lot of theory at this point so perhaps it's time for us to make our first game! It's not going to be that much fun, seeing as you'll know the answer – but you can get your friends to play it to impress them with your coding know-how (unfortunately, it's still not all that fun even then!).

The game is simply going to get the player to guess the number it is thinking of and will then give clues to help them get there if they get it wrong.

```
CorrectNumber = 16
```

```
while True:

    GuessedNumber = int(input("Guess the number I'm thinking of!"))

    if GuessedNumber == CorrectNumber:

        print("Correct!")

        break

    elifGuessedNumber<CorrectNumber:

        print("Too low!")

        continue

    elifGuessedNumber>CorrectNumber:

        print("Too high!")

        continue

print("You WIN!!!")
```

Nesting Ifs and Loops

It is also possible to 'nest' your ifs and your loops in order to make even more elaborate programs that test multiple different conditions.

We already did this once when we put the 'if' inside the loop. However we can also put ifs inside ifs inside ifs if we want!

Chapter 11

Turtle

Turtle is a module for graphics. It is a part of Python. In Turtle there are many basic commands. When you program, the turtle will run in lines and shapes based on your programming. But it will only move if you program it. And to do that, you need to know these commands.

For every program, you need to write these three lines on the top:

Tog ot o Turtle, from turtle import* you press File, mode ('standard')

shape ('turtle') then New Window.

Turtle always starts off facing

right. This information will come

handy when programming

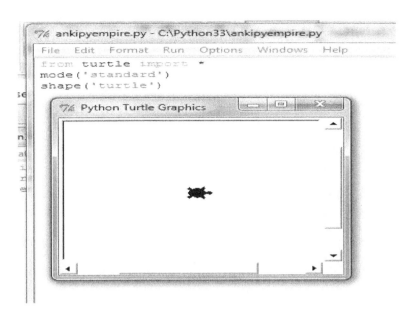

Without these lines, the program will not recognize most of the commands you use. Now, let us learn commands!

To make the turtle go forward, you write fd.

To make the turtle go backward, you write bk.

Now after you write fd, or bk, you put parenthesis and put a number inside that parenthesis. The number tells you how much you want to go forward or backward. For instance, if I wanted to go forward 100 units, then I wanted to go backward 250, the program would look like this:

from turtle import*

mode ('standard')

shape ('turtle')

fd(100)

bk(250)

Note how each command you type in will take up each one line. After you type this simple program, press the F5 key, or, in the menu bar, click on Run then Run Module on the drop-down to run this program. The program should go forward, then backward, because that was how we programmed it to be.

Now, to make it TURN right, you write rt. To make it TURN left, you write lt.

After you write rt or lt, you put parenthesis, and inside that you put the amount of degrees you want it to turn right or left. This is what your program might look now:

from turtle import*

mode ('standard')

shape ('turtle')

fd(100)

bk(250)

rt(90)

fd(100)

lt(90)

fd(100)

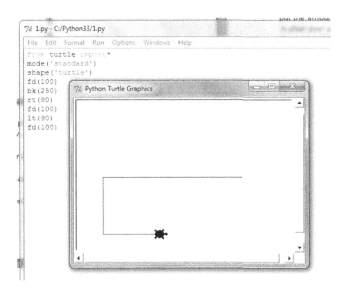

Another command you can use is home(). What this does is that it goes back to the starting point. For example, if you wanted to complete the shape you were making, you might want to add home() after the last line of your program.

You can also change the color and thickness of the line by using pensize and pencolor

pensize() changes the thickness of the line (you probably guessed). You can put a number in the parenthesis, and the thickness will change accordingly (the bigger the number, the bigger the line).

pencolor() changes the color of the line (you might have guessed that too). You can write a color in the parenthesis, and your line will become that color.

For example, if you wanted to make a blue square with thicker lines, the program would be like this:

from turtle import* mode('standard') shape('turtle') pencolor('blue')

pensize(25) read it as a command. This wayfd(100) you can make notes for yourselflt(90)

fd(100) on the program.lt (90)

fd(100)

lt(90)#it's turning left

fd(100)

If you put a hashtag (#) in front

of a command, Python will not

The outcome would be this:

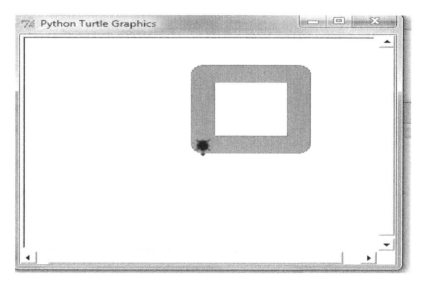

You can also tell the turtle not to make a line while moving. You can do that by using penup and pendown.

penup() will pick up the turtle. The turtle will move but not make any lines. You do not put anything in the parenthesis.

pendown() will return the turtle back to its regular line-making mode. You do not have to put anything inside the parenthesis.

Note: If you want Python to continue making lines, you have to write pendown after you write the penup.

You learned how to make straight lines in Python, right? So now the question is: Can you draw a circle?

Well of course!! All you do is write circle, add a parenthesis, and inside that, write the radius of the circle. The radius is the length of the exact center of the circle to a side of the circle.

The radius is a number. For example, if I wanted to make a large circle, I would write: circle(85) and for a small circle: circle(15)

Okay, so you know how to make lines on Python, and with those lines you can create shapes like squares, rectangles, and stars. You know how to go to home, change the color, thickness, and how to make a circle. What if I wanted to make my circle fancy and color in the circle?

Let us do it!

In the beginning of where you want to start filling in your shape or circle, you write begin_fill. After that, you have to write what color you want it to be filled in. To do that, you write fillcolor, parenthesis, and inside the parenthesis the color. Remember, since the color you want will be a word, you have to put single quotes around it. Ex) fillcolor('blue')

And wherever you want the shape to be filled, after you create the shape write end_fill. Here is an example:

from turtle import* mode ('standard') shape ('turtle') begin_fill()

fillcolor('pink') circle(100)

end_fill()

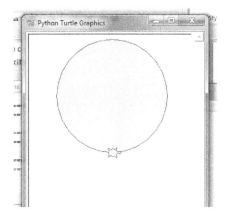

TA-DA!!! Now you know some basic commands for Python. With these commands, you can make a lot of shapes and lines. You might even be able to "make" the Eiffel Tower with them too! Python is easy and fun, and once you think you got the hang of these commands, learn the more complicate ones, and you will become a pro!

Here is a program for Hexagon

```
from turtle import *

mode('standard')

shape('turtle')

pencolor('blue')

write('This is Hexagon...')

pencolor('yellow')

pensize(5)

begin_fill()

fillcolor('red')

fd(50)

lt(60)

fd(50)

lt(60)

fd(50)
```

lt(60)

fd(50)

lt(60)

fd(50)

lt(60)

home()

end_fill()hideturtle()

Chapter 12

Fun Activities

Activity 1: How old are you?

So, we have introduced ourselves to the computer. Now, let us add to our introduction and tell it how old we are.

What to Do

Change your existing **print()** function (the one where you introduced yourself to the computer) to use an f-string (see here for the lesson that will help you do this). Create two variables: one called **name** and one called **age**. Assign a string with your name to the **name** variable. Assign a math operation (that equals your age) to the **age** variable. For example:

age = 20 + 7

Finally, print out your new introduction to the computer using your f-string and **name** and **age** variables!

Sample Expected Output

"Hi! My name is Adrienne and I am 27 years old!"

Activity 2: Cookie Comparison

Say you and your friends are eating some chocolate chip cookies. While you are all happily snacking away, one of your friends says, "My chocolate chip cookie has the most chocolate chips!" You think to yourself, "I think mine does." And now your other friends are curious, and look down at their chocolate chip cookies to see how their cookies compare with their friends'. How can you use coding to confirm whose claim is **True**? Who has more or less chocolate chips in their cookie between you and your friend; and how about among your other friends?

We could write a small program to help us make that decision. Let us do it!

Imagine that we built an awesome machine that was able to scan some cookies and then give you variables with the number of chocolate chips each contained. How would you use comparison operators to help you decide?

What to Do

For each pair of friends, write a **print()** function that outputs the two friends' chocolate chip numbers, the comparison you are using, and if it is **True**. Here is an example:

Dolores and Teddy both have cookies. Teddy thinks his cookie has more chocolate chips than Dolores's cookie. Of course, Dolores thinks the opposite. Let us see who is right.

Beep boop scanning noise

Great! We have scanned their cookies, and this is what is given to us by our cookie scanning machine:

dolores_chocolate_chips = 13

teddy_chocolate_chips = 9

Teddy thinks he has more chocolate chips in his cookie than Dolores does in hers. How would we write that comparison in code?

teddy_chocolate_chips>dolores_chocolate_chips

Exactly! Teddy thinks he has more chocolate chips than Dolores, so we use the greater-than operator (>). Now, how would we print out the results of this chocolate chip battle, including the comparison we are making? Hint: We can use f-strings! And another hint: full code comparisons can be used in the same way as variables!

print(f"Teddy's cookie has more chocolate chips than Dolores's. This is {teddy_chocolate_chips>dolores_chocolate_chips}!")

Awesome! It is kind of long, but it works!

Here are some more friends you need to help! Write a similar **print()** function for each pair of friends and their claim:

Rey and Finn

Rey says she has less than or equal to the number of chocolate chips as Finn.

rey_chocolate_chips = 10

finn_chocolate_chips = 18

Tom and Jerry

Tom says he does not have the same amount of chocolate chips in his cookie as Jerry.

tom_chocolate_chips = 50

jerry_chocolate_chips = "50"

Trinity and Neo

Neo says he has the same number of chocolate chips as Trinity.

neo_chocolate_chips = 3

trinity_chocolate_chips = 3

Gigi and Kiki

Kiki says she has less chocolate chips in her cookie than Gigi.

kiki_chocolate_chips = 30

gigi_chocolate_chips = 31

Bernard and Elsie

Bernard says he has at least the same amount of chocolate chips as Elsie, maybe even more!

bernard_chocolate_chips = 1010

elsie_chocolate_chips = 10101

Activity 3: Pie Party!

Today's our lucky day. We get to help the best baker in town prepare for the pie party! Baker Miguel wants to know how many of each kind of pie to bake to make sure everyone gets a slice that they like. We have some information available, but you will have to write some code to figure out exactly how many pies, and which pies, to bake!

Here is the information we know:

total_people = 124

graham_cracker_crust_lovers = 40

vanilla_wafer_crust_lovers = 64

oreo_crust_lovers = 20

Pie Types

Chocolate and Caramel Pie

pie_crust = "graham cracker"

pie_slices = 10

Triple Berry Pie

pie_crust = "vanilla wafer"

pie_slices = 12

Pumpkin Pie

pie_crust = "graham cracker"

pie_slices = 12

Apple Pie

pie_crust = "vanilla wafer"

pie_slices = 10

Banana Cream Pie

pie_crust = "vanilla wafer"

pie_slices = 10

Mango Pie

pie_crust = "graham cracker"

pie_slices = 12

S'mores Pie

pie_crust = "oreo"

pie_slices = 12

What to Do

Using logical operators, the **print()** function, and f-strings, write some code for each type of pie that determines if you can evenly divide the number of slices that type of pie has by the total number of people in that particular crust lovers' group!

Sample Expected Output

'The Chocolate and Caramel pie can be evenly divided for all Graham Crust Lovers? True'

Activity 4: Outfit Checker

Cher and Dionne are about to go to a fancy party. Being the fashionistas they are, they want to make sure their outfits aren't the same, but a few things in common are okay, especially since they both love pink! Let us write some code to make sure their outfits are as individual as they are!

What to Do

Using the variables provided, your knowledge of the **print()** function, and the proper logical operators, write code to help you check Cher and Dionne's outfits! Here are some variables that describe each girl's outfit:

cher_dress_color = 'pink'

cher_shoe_color = 'white'

cher_has_earrings = True

dionne_dress_color = 'purple'

dionne_shoe_color = 'pink'

dionne_has_earrings = True

For each outfit check, first determine which variables to use that best match the scenario. Then, write some code to compare the variables you have chosen with the proper logical operator. Finally, use the **print()** function to print a sentence stating the outfit check and use your comparison code as a **True** or **False** answer.

Example Outfit Check

At least one person is wearing purple.

Best matching variables to use for this outfit check:

cher_dress_color, dionne_dress_color

Choose a logical operator that allows you to test the condition in the outfit check. For this one, we only need to make sure that at least one person is wearing purple (at least one expression was **True**), so using the **or** operator is probably best.

Finally, use that comparison code to print the answer to the outfit check!

print(f"At least one person is wearing purple? {code to check that either cher or dionne's dress is purple}")

Example Output:

At least one person is wearing purple? True

Outfit Check 1

Cher and Dionne have different dress colors.

Outfit Check 2

Cher and Dionne are both wearing earrings.

Outfit Check 3

At least one person is wearing pink.

Outfit Check 4

No one is wearing green.

Outfit Check 5

Cher and Dionne have the same shoe color.

Sample Expected Output

Cher and Dionne have matching dress colors? False

Someone is wearing pink? True

Activity 5: Logical Lab

We have learned about the three sets of operators used in Python: arithmetic, logical, and comparison. This will come in handy now, because Ada needs our help sorting through her lab materials.

What to Do

Create a new file called adas-materials-report and save it. Then, declare the following variables:

beakers = 20

tubes = 30

rubber_gloves = 10

safety_glasses = 4

Ada has three friends coming to her lab to help her out, so you will need to determine if there are enough materials for each friend. To safely run some experiments, each friend needs to have:

1 pair of safety glasses

2 rubber gloves

5 beakers

10 tubes

Knowing this, create new variables to hold a Boolean value (**True** or **False**) determining if there are enough items for all the scientists:

enough_safety_glasses = <Write some code here!>

enough_rubber_gloves = <Write some code here!>

enough_tubes = <Write some code here!>

enough_beakers = <Write some code here!>

In the placeholders that say **<Write some code here!>**, write code that uses different arithmetic operators first to figure out if each friend will receive the proper amount of materials. Next, combine that code with some comparison operators to result in either a **True** or **False** answer. This will be the Boolean you assign to your "enough lab materials" variables.

Finally, once you have Booleans assigned to your variables, use them with logical operators to determine the following scenarios:

•There are enough gloves and safety glasses for each girl.

•There are enough tubes or enough beakers for each girl.

•Each girl has enough safety glasses and beakers or enough tubes and beakers.

•Each girl has enough gloves, safety glasses, tubes, and beakers.

For example, in the first scenario, "There are enough gloves and safety glasses for each girl," we can use the **enough_rubber_gloves** and

enough_safety_glasses variables for comparison with the **and** operator to check for the scenario's conditions.

Put all of this information together in a **final_report** variable:

final_report = f'''

Here is the final report for lab materials:

-

Each girl has enough safety glasses: {add the right variable here}

Each girl has enough rubber gloves: {add the right variable here}

Each girl has enough tubes: {add the right variable here}

Each girl has enough beakers: {add the right variable here}

-

There are enough gloves and safety glasses for each girl: {write some code here}

There are enough tubes and or enough beakers for each girl: {write some code here}

Each girl has enough safety glasses and beakers or enough tubes and beakers: {write some code here}

Each girl has enough gloves, safety glasses, tubes, and beakers: {write some code here}

'''

Use this variable in your **print()** function (be sure to fill in the blanks with the information you figured out above) to see the results!

Activity 6: Planetary Exponentiation

Scientist Angie needs our help! She has been exploring other galaxies and has been comparing how many planets they have to the nine that we have in our solar system (because even though it's a dwarf planet, she wants to include Pluto). Can you write some code to help her calculate the total planets for the other galaxies?

What to Do

Use the exponentiation operator to print out the total number of planets the other galaxies have. To do this, take our total number of planets and raise it to the power of each galaxy's magic number. Be sure to use the **total_planets** variable provided for your calculations!

total_planets = 9

Example Galaxy

In the Pentatopia galaxy, their magic number is 5. Write a **print()** function that prints out how many planets the Pentatopia galaxy has!

Sample Code

print(f"ThePentatopia galaxy has {write code to calculate what 9 to the power of 5 is} planets!")

Sample Output

The Pentatopia galaxy has 59049 planets!

Angie's Galaxy Research

In the **Tripolia galaxy**, their magic number is 3. Write a **print()** function that prints out how many planets the Tripolia galaxy has.

In the **Deka galaxy**, their magic number is 10. Write a **print()** function that prints out how many planets the Deka galaxy has.

In the **Heptaton galaxy**, their magic number is 7. Write a **print()** function that prints out how many planets the Heptaton galaxy has.

In the **Oktopia galaxy**, their magic number is 8. Write a **print()** function that prints out how many planets the Oktopia galaxy has.

Activity 7 : Finding the sum of 1 + 2 + 3 + … + 100

Write a Python program that calculates and displays the following sum:S = 1 + 2 + 3 + … + 100

What to Do

This exercise can be solved using a sequence structure. Not the best option, but it is an option! Variable i increments from 1 to 100, and each time its value is accumulated in variable s.

s = 0

i = 1

s = s + i #this pair of statements must be written 100 times.

i = i + 1

s = s + i

i = i + 1

s = s + i

i = i + 1

print(s)

Obviously, you can do the same using a while structure that increments variable i from 1 to 100. In each iteration, its value is accumulated in variable s.

file_ 22 _1 _1 a

s = 0

i = 1

while i<= 100:

s = s + i

i = i + 1

print(s)

Or you can do the same using a for structure, as shown here.

file_ 22 _1 _1 b

s = 0

for i in range(1, 101):

s = s + i

print(s)

Activity 8: Finding the product of 2 × 4 × 6 × 8 × 10

Write a Python program that calculates and displays the following product: P = 2 × 4 × 6 × 8 × 10

What to Do

Once again, this exercise can be solved using a sequence structure.

p = 1

i = 2

p = p * i

i = i + 2

p = p * i

i = i + 2

p = p * i

i = i + 2

p = p * i

i = i + 2

p = p * i

i = i + 2

print(p)

And once more, you can do the same using a while structure that increments variable i by 2, from 2 to 10.

file_ 22 _1 _2 a

p = 1

i = 2

while i<= 10:

p = p * i

i += 2

print(p)

Or you can even use a for structure, as shown here.

file_ 22 _1 _2 b

p = 1

for i in range(2, 12, 2):

p = p * i

print(p)

Activity 9: Finding the average value of positive numbers

Write a Python program that prompts the user to enter 100 numbers and thencalculates and displays the average value of the positive numbers.

What to Do

Since you know the total number of iterations, you can use a for structure.

Inside the loop, however, an if structure must check whether the given number is positive; if so, it must accumulate the given number in variable total. When the flow of execution exits the loop, the average value can then be calculated. The Python program is as follows.

file_ 22 _1 _3 a

```
total = 0
count = 0
for i in range(100):
    x = float(input( "Enter a number: " ))
    if x > 0:
        total += x
        count += 1
if count != 0:
```

print(total / count)

else:

print("No positives entered!")

Activity 10: Counting the numbers according to which is greater

Write a Python program that prompts the user to enter 10 pairs of numbers and then counts and displays the number of times that the first number of a given pair was greater than the second number.

What to Do

Once again, a for structure can be used. The Python program is as follows.

file_ 22 _1 _4 b

count_a = 0

count_b = 0

for i in range(10):

a = int(input("Enter number A: "))

b = int(input("Enter number B: "))

if a > b:

count_a += 1

elif b > a:

count_b += 1

print(count_a, count_b)

A reasonable question that someone may ask is "Why is an if-elif structure being used here? Why not use an if-else structure instead? " Suppose that an if-else structure such as the following is used.

if a > b:

count_a += 1

else:

count_b += 1

In this decision structure, the variable count_b increments when variable b is greater than variable a (this is desirable) but also when variable b is equal to variable a (this is undesirable). Using an if-elif structure instead ensures that variable count_b increments only when variable b is greater than (and not when it is equal to) variable a.

Activity 11: Counting the numbers according to their digits

Write a Python program that prompts the user to enter 20 integers. The program then counts and displays three different results: the number of one-digit integers that were given, the number of two-digit integers, and the number of three-digit integers. Assume that the user enters values between 1 and 999.

What to Do

Nothing new here! The Python program is as follows.

file_ 22 _1 _5

count1 = 0

count2 = 0

count3 = 0

for i in range(20):

a = int(input("Enter a number: "))

if a <= 9:

count1 += 1

elif a <= 99:

count2 += 1

else:

count3 += 1

print(count1, count2, count3)

Activity 12: How many numbers fit in a sum

Write a Python program that prompts the user to enter numeric values repeatedly until their sum exceeds 1000. At the end, the program must display the total quantity of numbers entered.

What to Do

In this case, you do not know the exact number of iterations, so you cannot use a for structure. Let's use a while structure instead, but, in order to make your program free of logic errors you should follow the "Ultimate" rule: the while structure that solves this problem should be as follows.

total = 0 #Initialization of total

while total <= 1000: #A Boolean expression dependent on total

Here goes

a statement or block of statements

total += x #Update/alteration of total

The only statements that are missing are the statement that prompts the user to enter a number, and the statement that counts the numbers entered. The final Python program becomes

file_ 22 _1 _6

count = 0 #This is not here due to the Ultimate Rule!

total = 0

while total <= 1000:

x = float(input("Enter a number: "))

count += 1

total += x

print(count)

Activity 13: Iterating as many times as the user wants

Write a Python program that prompts the user to enter two numbers. It thencalculates and displays the result of the first number raised to the power of the

second one. The program must iterate as many times as the user wants. At the end of each calculation, the program must ask the user if they want to calculate the result of another pair of numbers. If the answer is "yes" the program must repeat; it must end otherwise. Make your program accept the answer in all possible forms, such as "yes", "YES", "Yes", or even "YeS".

What to Do

According to the "Ultimate" rule, the while structure should be as follows, given in general form.

answer = "yes" #Initialization of answer

while answer.upper() == "YES" :

Here goes the code that

prompts the user to enter two numbers and then

calculates and displays the first number

raised to the power of the second one.

#Update/alteration of answer

answer = input("Would you like to repeat? ")

The solution to this exercise becomes

file_ 22 _1 _7

```
answer = "yes" #Initialization of answer
while answer.upper() == "YES" :
    a = int(input( "Enter number A: " ))
    b = int(input( "Enter number B: " ))
    result = a ** b
    print( "The result is:" , result)
    answer = input( "Would you like to repeat? " )
```

Activity 14: Rice on a chessboard

There is a myth about a poor man who invented chess. The King of India was so pleased with that new game that he offered to give the poor man anything he wished for. The poor but wise man told his King that he would like one grain of rice for the first square of the board, two grains for the second, four grains for the third and so on, doubled for each of the 64 squares of the game board. This seemed tithe King to be a modest request, so he ordered his servants to bring the rice.

Write a Python program that calculates how many grains of rice will be on the chessboard in the end.

What to Do

Assume a chessboard of only 2 × 2 = 4 squares and a variable grains assigned the initial value 1 (this is the number of grains of the 1st square). A for structure that iterates three times can double the value of variable grains in each iteration, as shown in the next code fragment.

grains = 1

for i in range(3):

grains = 2 * grains

The value of the variable grains at the end of each iteration is shown in the next table.

Iteration

Value of variable grains

1st

2 × 1 = **2**

2nd

2 × 2 = **4**

3rd

2 × 4 = **8**

At the end of the 3rd iteration, the variable grains contain the value 8. This value, however, is not the total number of grains on the chessboard but only the number of grains on the 4th square. If you need to find the total number of grains on the chessboard you can sum up the grains on all squares, that is, 1 + 2 + 4 + 8 = 15.

In the real world a real chessboard contains 8 × 8 = 64 squares, thus you need to iterate for 63 times. The Python program is as follows.

file_ 22 _1 _10

```
grains = 1
total = 1
for i in range(63):
    grains = 2 * grains
    total = total + grains
print(total)
```

In case you are wondering how big this number is, here is your answer: On the chessboard there will be 18,446,744,073,709,551,615 grains of rice!

Activity 15: Find the secret number

Write a Python program that assigns a random secret integer between 1 and 100 to a variable and then prompts the user to guess the number. If the integer given is greater than the secret one, a message "Your guess is bigger than my secret number. Try again." must be displayed. If the integer given is less than the secret one, a message "Your guess is smaller than my secret number. Try again." must be displayed. This must repeat until the user finally finds the secret number. Then, a message "You found it!" must be displayed, as well as the total number of the user's attempts.

What to Do

According to the "Ultimate" rule, the while structure should be as follows, given in general form.

guess = int(input("Enter a guess: ")) #Initialization of guess while guess != secret_number:

Here goes the rest of the code

#Update/alteration of guess

guess = int(input("Enter a guess: "))

The rest of the code that goes into the while structure is quite easy. More precisely, the user's guess must be compared to the secret number and proper messages must be displayed. Also, the variable that holds the user's attempts must be increased by 1.

Sample Code

file_ 22 _1 _11

import random

secret_number = random.randrange(1, 101)

```
attempts = 1
guess = int(input( "Enter a guess: " ))
while guess != secret_number:
    if guess >secret_number:
        print( "Your guess is bigger than my secret number. Try again." )
    else:
        print( "Your guess is smaller than my secret number. Try again." )
    attempts += 1
    guess = int(input( "Enter a guess: " ))
print( "You found it!" )
print( "Attempts:" , attempts)
```

Chapter 13

Learning Games

Rock Paper scissors

The first game will be Rock Paper Scissors, which is normally played by two people, but in this case it's going to be you against the computer. The first thing we need to do when creating a game is brainstorming. Take a pen and paper and think about how the game should be designed. Start by first considering the rules of the game, and only then worry about the programming side.

This classic game involves choosing one of three objects, as the name suggests. Once both selections are made, the items are revealed to see who wins. The player who wins is determined by three simple rules.

The rock will crush the scissors, while the scissors cut paper and the paper covers rock.

To handle these rules we are going to create a list of choices, similar to the list of colors we created before in some of our drawing programs. Then we will add a random selection function that will represent the choice the computer makes. Next, the human player will have to make his or her choice. Finally, the winner is decided with the help of a number of if statements.

Have you tried to create your own version of the game yet? If so, good job! Even if you didn't completely finish it or you wrote the game and you're getting some errors, you should still reward yourself for trying. Now, let's go through the code and see how this game should turn out:

```
import random

selectionChoices = [ "rock", "paper", "scissors"]

print ("Rock beats scissors. Scissors cut paper. Paper covers rock.")

player = input ("Do you want to choose rock, paper, or scissors? (or quit) ?"

while player != "quit":

    player = player.lower ()

computer  =   random.choice(selectionChoices)

print("You selected " +player+ ",
```

```
and the   computer   selected"    +computer+ ".")
if player == computer:
print("Draw!")
elif  player == "rock":
if computer == "scissors":
print ("Victory!")
else:
print("You lose!")
elif  player == "paper":
if computer == "rock":
print("Victory!")
    else:
print("You lose!")
elif  player  == "scissors":
if computer == "paper":
print
("Victory!")
    else:
print("You lose!")
else:
```

print("Something went wrong...")

print()

player = input ("Do you want to choose rock, paper, or scissors? (or quit) ?"

Discussion

First we import the random package which allows us to use a number of functions that we are going to take advantage of when giving the computer the ability to make random choices. Then we create a list for the three game objects and print the games rules so that the human player knows them. The computer will already know what to do because it is programmed, after all. Next, we ask the player to type his or her choice and then a loop is executed to check the choice of the player. The player also has the option of quitting the prompt window, and when that happens the game is over. Our loop makes sure that if the player doesn't select the quit option, the game will run.

The next step is to ask the computer to select one of the three game objects. This choice is done randomly and the selected item is stored inside a variable called "computer". After the choice is memorized, the testing phase begins to see which player will win. First a check is performed to see whether the two players have chosen the same item. If they did, then the result is a draw and nobody wins. Next, the program verifies whether the player chose rock, and then it looks at the computer to see if it chose scissors. If this is the case, then the rule says rock beats scissors, so the player wins. If the computer didn't select a rock as well, neither did it pick scissors, then it certainly chose paper. In this case the computer will win. Next, we have two elif statements where we perform two more tests that check whether the player selected paper or scissors. Here we also have a statement that checks to see if the player chose something that isn't one of the three possible items. If that is the case, an error message is sent that tells the player he either chose something that he is not allowed, or he mistyped the command.

Lastly, the user is prompted to type the next selection. This is where the main loop goes back to the beginning. In other words, the game starts another round of rock paper scissors.

This game is simple, but it is fun because anyone can win. The computer has a chance of beating you and there's also a real chance of ending up in a draw. Now that you understand how to create a random chance type of game, let's look at other examples to add to our game library while also learning Python programming.

Guessing Game

This project will be another fun chance based game that will make use of the random module. The purpose of the game will be choosing a number between a minimum and a maximum and then the opponent tries to guess that number. If the player guesses a higher number, he will have to try a smaller one, and the other way around as well. Only a perfect match will turn into a win.

Comparing numbers is something we already did, by using the if statement. We have also used the input function to interact with the program and we are going to make use of it here once again. In addition, we will need a while loop as well.

In this project the random module is needed because of certain specific functions. For instance, we know that we need to generate a random number, therefore we will use a function called "randint" which stands for random integer. The function will have two parameters, which represent the minimum number we can have, as well as the maximum.

You can try out this function on its own. Just import the module and then type the following:

import random

random.randint (1, 20)

Python will now automatically generate a random figure between 1 and 20. Keep in mind that the minimum and maximum values are included in the number generation, therefore Python can also generate numbers 1 or 20. You can test this command as many times as you want to make sure that you are truly getting random values. If you execute it often enough, you will see that some values will repeat themselves, and if the range is large enough you might not even encounter certain numbers no matter how many times you run the code. What's interesting about this function though, is that it isn't truly random. This is just a side note that won't affect your program, but it is intriguing nonetheless. The randint function actually follows a specific pattern and the chosen numbers only appear to be random, but they aren't. Python follows a complex algorithm for this pattern instead, and therefore we experience the illusion of randomness. With that being said, let's get back to fun and games. Let's create our game with the following code:

import random

randomNumbers = random.randint (1, 100)

myGuess = int (input ("Try to guess the number. It can be anywhere from 1 to 100:"))

while guess != randomNumbers:

    if myGuess>randomNumbers:

        print (myGuess, "was larger than the number. Guess again!"

    if myGuess<randomNumbers:

        print (myGuess, "was smaller than the number. Guess again!"

myGuess = int (input ("Try and guess again! "))

print (myGuess, "you got it right! You won!")

That's it! Hopefully you tried to create this game on your own because you already have the tools for the job. Remember that programming is only easy as long as you practice it enough on your own. Just take it one step at a time. With that being said, let's discuss the code in case you need some help figuring the game out:

Just like before, we first need to import the random module so that we can use the random number generating function. Next, we use the randint function with two parameters. As mentioned before, these parameters are the lowest number we can guess, which is 1, and the highest number we can guess, 100. The random number generator will generate a number within this range. Once the number is generated, it is stored inside the "randomNumbers" variable which we declared. This number will not be known by the player because he or she needs to guess it. That's the point of the game.

Next up, the player needs to guess the hidden number. This guess will then be stored inside a new variable called "myGuess". In order to check whether the guess is equal to the number, we are using a while loop with the "not equal to" operator. We do this because if the player gets lucky and guesses the number correctly with the first attempt, the loop simply doesn't finish executing because there's no need.

Next, if the player guesses the wrong number, we have two if statements that check whether the guess is a higher value than the hidden number, or a lower one. An appropriate message is then printed for the player in each case. In either scenario, the player receives another chance to make the right guess. Finally, at the end if the user guessed the number correctly, the program declares victory by printing a message and then the program stops running.

Choose a Card

Card games are always fun and they also rely on random elements to some degree. No matter the card game, chances are quite small to have multiple identical games. This means you won't get bored any time soon. We can create a card game. It might not look good, unless you have an artistic friend to draw everything for you, but you could still create the graphics with the help of the Turtle module like we did for other projects. This will require some patience though. In any case, we can create a card game even without graphics by simply generating the name of each card. Instead of seeing a virtual card, we will see the name "four of spades", or "queen of hearts".

Before we continue, you should take note that this project is your challenge. You have learned everything you need to write such a game, and we already created two other fairly similar projects. So this time, you are almost entirely on your own. As usual, start with a pen and paper and figure everything out logically. Worry about the code afterwards. However, to help you out a little, we are going to brainstorm together just to give you some ideas.

One of the simplest card games we could create involves a game with two players that battle each other to see who draws the card with the highest value. Each player will randomly pull a card from the deck, and the one who has the higher card will win. It is a simple game, but fun due to the random element.

Since we won't be using any graphics, we will have to create our deck of cards some other way. We are going to set them all up as a list of strings since we will be using their names instead. Next, we need to give the players the ability to pull a card from the deck randomly. This means that we are going to use the random module once again and we will add a choice function that randomly distributes cards to the players. Finally, we need a way to compare the two cards that are drawn by the two players. As you probably guessed, this is a case for comparison operators.

Full Code:

```
Import time, os, random
ranks= ["Ace","2","3","4","5","6","7","8","9","10","Jack","Queen","King"]
suits= ["Clubs","Hearts","Diamonds","Spades"]
deck= []
```

```
value=1
for rank in ranks:
    for suit in suits:
        deck.append([rank+" of "+suit, value])
        value=value+1
random.shuffle(deck)
score=0
card1=deck.pop(0)
while True:
    os.system("cls") # linux "clear"
    print("Your score so far is", score)
    print("\n\nThe current card is", card1[0])
    while True:
        choice=input("higher or lower?")
        if len(choice) >0:
            if choice[0].lower() in ["h","l"]:
                break
    card2=deck.pop(0)
    print("The next card picked is", card2[0])
    time.sleep(1)
    if choice[0].lower() =="h" and card2[1] >card1[1]:
        print("Correct!")
```

```
score+=1
time.sleep(1)
ifchoice[0].lower() =="h"andcard2[1] <card1[1]:
print("Wrong!")
time.sleep(1)
break
ifchoice[0].lower() =="l"andcard2[1] <card1[1]:
print("Correct!")
score+=1
time.sleep(1)
ifchoice[0].lower() =="l"andcard2[1] >card1[1]:
print("Wrong!")
time.sleep(1)
break
else:
print("draw!")
card1=card2
os.system("cls")
print("Game over!")
print("You final score is", score)
time.sleep(4)
os.system("cls")
```

Chapter 14

Advance Games

Creating Your Skier Game

Skier (and a number of games) uses a Pygame module to help create games for your game. The module comes with a Python when it's installed. But just in case you don't have it installed alongside your Python yet, you can get it from www.pygame.org right away. You'll also need some skier customized graphic files that'll be used for your game.

1. skier_down.png
2. skier_right1.png
3. skier_right2.png
4. skier_left1.png
5. skier_left2.png
6. skier_crash.png
7. skier_tree.png
8. skier_flag.png

9. They should be put in the same directory or path as the original program for easy access. Here's the code (that's a bit long, but not impossible).

10. import pygame, sys, random

11. skier_images = ["skier_down.png", "skier_right1.png",

    a. "skier_right2.png", "skier_left2.png",

    b. "skier_left1.png"]

12. class SkierClass(pygame.sprite.Sprite):

13. def __init__(self):

14. pygame.sprite.Sprite.__init__(self)

15. self.image = pygame.image.load("skier_down.png")

16. self.rect = self.image.get_rect()

17. self.rect.center = [320, 100]

18. self.angle = 0

19. def turn(self, direction):

20. self.angle = self.angle + direction

21. if self.angle< -2: self.angle = -2

22. if self.angle> 2: self.angle = 2

23. center = self.rect.center

24. self.image = pygame.image.load(skier_images[self.angle])

25. self.rect = self.image.get_rect()

26. self.rect.center = center

27. speed = [self.angle, 6 - abs(self.angle) * 2]

28. return speed

29. def move(self, speed):

30. self.rect.centerx = self.rect.centerx + speed[0]

31. if self.rect.centerx< 20: self.rect.centerx = 20

32. if self.rect.centerx> 620: self.rect.centerx = 620

33. class ObstacleClass(pygame.sprite.Sprite):

34. def __init__(self, image_file, location, type):

35. pygame.sprite.Sprite.__init__(self)

36. self.image_file = image_file

37. self.image = pygame.image.load(image_file)

38. self.rect = self.image.get_rect()

39. self.rect.center = location

40. self.type = type

41. self.passed = False

42. def update(self):

43. global speed

44. self.rect.centery -= speed[1]

45. if self.rect.centery< -32:

46. self.kill()

47. def create_map():

48. global obstacles

49. locations = []

50. for i in range(10):

51. row = random.randint(0, 9)

52. col = random.randint(0, 9)

53. location = [col * 64 + 20, row * 64 + 20 + 640]

54. if not (location in locations):

55. locations.append(location)

56. type = random.choice(["tree", "flag"])

57. if type == "tree": img = "skier_tree.png"

58. elif type == "flag": img = "skier_flag.png"

59. obstacle = ObstacleClass(img, location, type)

60. obstacles.add(obstacle)

61. def animate():

62. screen.fill([255, 255, 255])

63. obstacles.draw(screen)

64. screen.blit(skier.image, skier.rect)

65. screen.blit(score_text, [10, 10])

66. pygame.display.flip()

67. pygame.init()

68. screen = pygame.display.set_mode([640,640])

69. clock = pygame.time.Clock()

70. skier = SkierClass()

71. speed = [0, 6]

72. obstacles = pygame.sprite.Group()

73. map_position = 0

74. points = 0

75. create_map()

76. font = pygame.font.Font(None, 50)

77. running = True

78. while running:

79. clock.tick(30)

80. for event in pygame.event.get():

81. if event.type == pygame.QUIT:

82. running = False

83. if event.type == pygame.KEYDOWN:

    a. if event.key == pygame.K_LEFT:

        i. speed = skier.turn(-1)

    b. elifevent.key == pygame.K_RIGHT:

        i. speed = skier.turn(1)

84. skier.move(speed)

85. map_position += speed[1]

86. if map_position>= 640:

87. create_map()

88. map_position = 0

89. hit = pygame.sprite.spritecollide(skier, obstacles, False)

90. if hit:

91. if hit[0].type == "tree" and not hit[0].passed:

92. points = points - 100

93. skier.image = pygame.image.load("skier_crash.png")

94. animate()

95. pygame.time.delay(1000)

96. skier.image = pygame.image.load("skier_down.png")

97. skier.angle = 0

98. speed = [0, 6]

99. hit[0].passed = True

100.   elifhit[0].type == "flag" and not hit[0].passed:

101.   points += 10

102.   hit[0].kill()

103.   obstacles.update()

104.   score_text = font.render("Score: " +str(points), 1, (0, 0, 0))

105.   animate()

106.   pygame.quit()

Try typing out your Python program with the right indentation. The whole code can be affected if you don't get it right. Most of the time, Python automatically helps you indent. But you still have to make sure they follow all the block code rules. The first step is making sure this code is typed in correctly, when you've done that, the rest is easy. Let's move to the next game.

Creating a Tic-Tac-Toe Game

This is a very common game that can even be played without a computer. It's sometimes referred to as the X-and-O game, and it usually requires two players (except you decide to play with your computer). For this exercise, however, we'll be creating one for two players. This particular game doesn't need any external or installed module to write the code. You can write it from virtually any Python code program that exists. Easy peasy! Just in case you haven't heard of the game until now, here's how it usually goes:

Two players are represented with the X and O symbols. Each player takes turns to put his symbol anywhere in a 3 by 3 game canvas. The whole aim is for a player to have this symbol appear three times either vertically, horizontally or diagonally. Each player tries blocking the other from getting this done. If, eventually, one player is able to get his three straight spaces, he wins, and the game is over. Usually, the game is played for a couple more rounds (until both players are tired) and there's a cumulative of who won the most rounds. If no one is able to get three straight symbol rows till all the tiles are filled, then no one wins that round and they move on to another. Tic-tac-toe is a fun game. Let's see how the code can be written.

1. **def** insertBoard(letter, pos):
2.   **global** board
3.   board[pos] = letter
4.
5.
6. **def** spaceIsFree(pos):
7.   **return** board[pos] == \' \'
8.
9.
10. **def** isWinner(bo, le):
    # Given a board and a player's letter, this function returns True if that player has won.
    # We use bo instead of board and le instead of letter so we don't have to type as much.
11.   **return** ((bo[7] == le **and** bo[8] == le **and** bo[9] == le) **or** # across the top
12.   (bo[4] == le **and** bo[5] == le **and** bo[6] == le) **or** # across the middle

13.   (bo[1] == le **and** bo[2] == le **and** bo[3] == le) **or** # across the bottom
14.   (bo[7] == le **and** bo[4] == le **and** bo[1] == le) **or** # down the left side
15.   (bo[8] == le **and** bo[5] == le **and** bo[2] == le) **or** # down the middle
16.   (bo[9] == le **and** bo[6] == le **and** bo[3] == le) **or** # down the right side
17.   (bo[7] == le **and** bo[5] == le **and** bo[3] == le) **or** # diagonal
18.   (bo[9] == le **and** bo[5] == le **and** bo[1] == le)) # diagonal
19.
20.
21. **def** playerMove():
22.   run = True
23.   **while** run:
24.   move = input(\'Please select a position to place an \\\'X\\\' (1-9): \')
25.   **try**:
26.   move = int(move)
27.   **if** move > 0 **and** move < 10:
28.   **if** spaceIsFree(move):
29.   run = False
30.   insertBoard(\'X\', move)

```
31.         else:
32.             print('This postion is already occupied!')
33.         else:
34.             print('Please type a number within the range!')
35.     except:
36.         print('Please type a number!')
37.
38.
39. def selectRandom(li):
40.     import random
41.     ln = len(li)
42.     r = random.randrange(0, ln)
43.     return li[r]
44.
45.
46. def compMove():
47.     possibleMoves = [x for x, letter in enumerate(board) if letter == ' ' and x != 0]
48.     move = 0
49.
        #Check for possible winning move to take or to block opponents winning move
50.     for let in ['O','X']:
```

```
51.     for i in possibleMoves:
52.         boardCopy = board[:]
53.         boardCopy[i] = let
54.         if isWinner(boardCopy, let):
55.             move = i
56.             return move
57.
58.
        #Try to take one of the corners
59.     cornersOpen = []
60.     for i in possibleMoves:
61.         if i in [1,3,7,9]:
62.             cornersOpen.append(i)
63.     if len(cornersOpen) > 0:
64.         move = selectRandom(cornersOpen)
65.         return move
66.
        #Try to take the center
67.     if 5 in possibleMoves:
68.         move = 5
69.         return move
70.
        #Take any edge
```

```
71.   edgesOpen = []
72.   for i in possibleMoves:
73.       if i in [2,4,6,8]:
74.           edgesOpen.append(i)
75.
76.   if len(edgesOpen) > 0:
77.       move = selectRandom(edgesOpen)
78.
79.   return move
80.
81.
82. def isBoardFull(board):
83.   if board.count(' ') > 1:
84.       return False
85.   else:
86.       return True
87.
88.
89. def printBoard():
      # "board" is a list of 10 strings representing the board (ignore index 0)
90.   print(' |   |')
91.   print(' ' + board[1] + ' | ' + board[2] + ' | ' + board[3])
```

92. **print**('| |')
93. **print**('-----------')
94. **print**('| |')
95. **print**(' ' + board[4] + ' | ' + board[5] + ' | ' + board[6])
96. **print**('| |')
97. **print**('-----------')
98. **print**('| |')
99. **print**(' ' + board[7] + ' | ' + board[8] + ' | ' + board[9])
100. **print**('| |')
101.
102.
103. **def** main():
     #Main game loop
104. **print**('Welcome to Tic Tac Toe, to win complete a straight line of your letter (Diagonal, Horizontal, Vertical). The board has positions 1-9 starting at the top left.')
105. printBoard()
106.
107. **while not**(isBoardFull(board)):
108.   **if not**(isWinner(board, 'O')):
109.   playerMove()
110.   printBoard()
111.   **else**:

```
112.            print(\'O\\\'s win this time...\')
113.            break
114.
115.
116.        if not(isWinner(board, \'X\')):
117.            move = compMove()
118.            if move == 0:
119.                print(\'Game is a Tie! No more spaces left to move.\')
120.            else:
121.                insertBoard(\'O\', move)
122.                print(\'Computer placed an \\\'O\\\' in position\', move, \':\')
123.                printBoard()
124.        else:
125.            print(\'X\\\'s win, good job!\')
126.            break
127.
128.
129.    if isBoardFull(board):
130.        print(\'Game is a tie! No more spaces left to move.\')
131.
132. main()
133.
```

134.   **while** True:
135.   answer = input(\'Do you want to play again? (Y/N)\')
136.   **if** answer.lower() == \'y\' **or** answer.lower == \'yes\':
137.   board = [\' \' **for** x **in** range(10)]
138.   print(\'-----------------------------------\')
139.   main()
140.   **else**:
141.   **break**

Once again, try your possible best to input this code in your IDLE shell correctly. If you run it, and it shows error messages, go back to the line that has the error and make corrections. If doesn't, then you know you've done right.

```
Type "copyright", "credits" or "license()" for more information.
>>>
============ RESTART: C:\Users\timot\Desktop\Tic Tac Toe\main.py ============
Welcome to Tic Tac Toe, to win complete a straight line of your letter (Diagonal
, Horizontal, Vertical). The board has positions 1-9 starting at the top left.
 |   |
 |   |
 |   |
-----------
 |   |
 |   |
 |   |
-----------
 |   |
 |   |
 |   |
Please select a position to place an 'X' (1-9): |
```

Sample output

Let's go ahead and get an explanation for the Tic-Tac-Toe, since it doesn't seem too complicated.

First, we define the game to include the board, end and win_combination elements. The board consists of a list from 1 to 9, which will eventually serve as the game board. The win_combination shows well, the possible winning combinations. There're eight of them. Under this defined function, we define another function draw that outputs the game board when we eventually run it. The next step is to define the elements of p1 (player one). You write a code that doesn't allow for a player to input his try on the spot where another player already has something. You do the same when you're defining a player too. Up next, you define another function that allows the user to choose a number between 1 and 9. If the number is not within the range, it sends a message that the number isn't available on the board. If the user enters anything asides a number, he is made to know that it isn't a number.

Next, you determine how a player wins the game, or not, based on the previous win combinations. If no one wins, the players are made to know that the game ends in a tie. The next set of code is that that instructs the different players at their turns to place their symbols. A special feature of the code is the last block that allows the different players to input their names for easy identification and more user-friendly. It also gives you the option of playing again if you wish, or else, it ends the game.

Running the code and playing the game is a lot of fun.

There are a million games in existence today. Some of them already put up their source code for whoever needs it. It's very advisable for beginners like you to search for this code, practice them in your own Python shell and see how the code works. With time, you get a hang of it and you begin to write your own codes (little by little) in no time.

Launching a ball at a random angle

We need to rewrite the __init__() function in the ball class like this:

def

   __init__(self):

   d=((math.pi/3)*random.random()+(math.pi/3))+math.pi*random.randint(0,1)

     self.dx=math.sin(d)*12

     self.dy=math.cos(d)*12

    self.x=475

    self.y=275

We've used the math and the random modules from Python so we have to import these on the first line:

import

   pygame, sys, math, random

Now, let's look at that "d" line:

    d=(math.pi/3)*random.random()+(math.pi/3)+math.pi*random.choice(0,1)

d is for direction and is going to be a the value of an angle in radians. It's not used outside the __init__() function so it doesn't need a "self".

We have to write math.pi rather than just pi because pi is only defined in Python's math module. This is why we loaded math in the first line.

The d variable is going to be the angle at which the ball sets off. We want the angle to be roughly towards the left or right side of the screen, not up or down. something in this region:

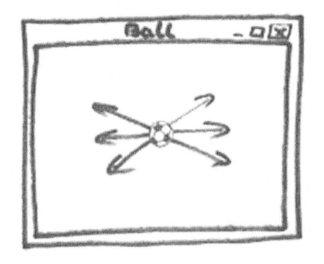

The first bit, math.pi/3, gives us an angle.

Remember that y is positive going down and x is positive to the right. So an angle of zero is pointing down and goes positive as it turns counter clockwise.

If we launch the ball at an angle of pi/3 this is the direction it would go:

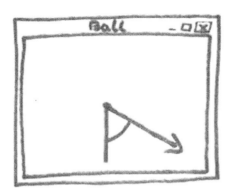

random.random() gives us a number between 0 and 1. For example, we might get 0.54 or 0.27. (Though, being python, it will be to a zillion decimal places.)

So math.pi/3*random.random() gives us an angle somewhere between 0 and pi/3 radians. (That's between 0 and 60 degrees.)

So if we launch a ball at this angle it will go somewhere in this direction:

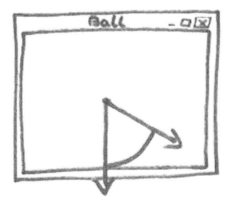

Next we add pi/3 radians. This will shift the range of angles like so:

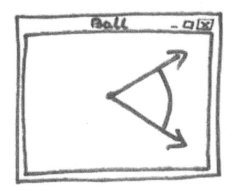

In the final part of the line the random.choice() function chooses a random integer from the list in the parenthesis. (We used this to randomise the speed of the badguy.) Here we are choosing from 0 or 1.

math.pi*random.choice(0,1,) will randomly choose either 0 times pi or 1 times pi. We then add this onto the angle. (This is like adding either 0 degrees or 180 degrees.)

So we get an angle d that's somewhere in the following range:

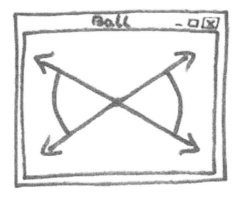

So far we haven't actually mentioned radians. We just have a number somewhere between 0 and 2pi.

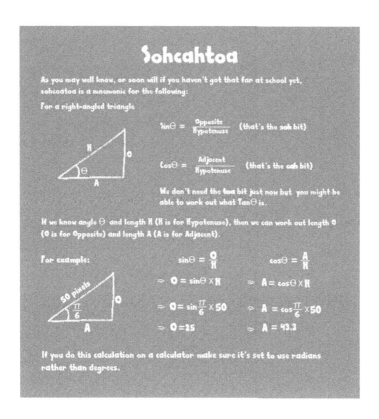

We want the ball to move 12 pixels in the chosen direction. But Python moves things in either the x direction or the y direction. To move at angles we have to combine the two.

self.dx=math.sin(d)*12

self.dy=math.cos(d)*12

Once we know angle d we can use Sohcoatoa (coming right up) to set the change in the x and y values. That is to find dx and dy.

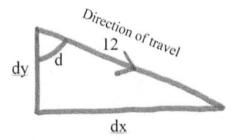

We know angle d because we've just set it. The length of the hypotenuse is the number of pixels we want the ball to move in each loop. 12 in this case.

dx is the Opposite.

dy is the Adjacent.

Here zero is pointing down. In the programming notes coming up the zero is to the right.

dx = sin d x 12

and

dy = cos d x 12

So there we have it. We set an angle that's not completely random but has some randomness in it, then use some basic maths to work out dy and dx.

This code we have worked on is commonly used. You'll be able to cut and paste it into other projects.

We could have used it to launch the space invaders. For example, the __init__() function from the badguy class here could look like this:

```
def __init__(self):

    self.x = random.randint(0,570)

    self.y = -100

    d=(math.pi/2)*random.random()-(math.pi/4)

    speed = random.randint(2,6)
```

self.dx=math.sin(d)*speed

self.dy=math.cos(d)*speed

(Making sure to add in math to the list of imports on line 1) Try it. It works just as well as our method before.)

(Math.pi/2)*random.random() gets our range of angle. (pi/2 radians is 90 degrees)

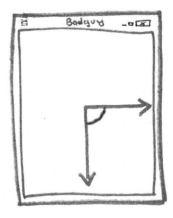

-(math.pi/4) rotates the range of angle to point down.

We're taking pi/4 radians off the angle. This effectively rotates the angle clockwise.

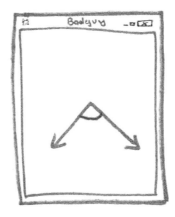

We set a random speed. Then we use sohcahtoa to find dx and dy.

We've set the starting point to 100 pixels above the screen and a random number between 0 and 570 on the x axis.

And so, together with the move() and bounce() functions, we should get bad guys coming down at random angles like this:

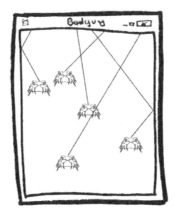

Conclusion

This is the end of your introduction to the basis of Python. Coding is all around us. Teaching a young child how to code sounds complicated, especially when we as adults don't always understand it, but all we need to do is take it right back to basics. For example, if they are interested in robotics, then finding a website or program that teaches Arduino may be preferable. If their interest lies in building websites, then look for courses that teach HTML or CSS. Your child may not ever want to work with computers, but who knows what we want to do when we are an adult, really? Your child's dream job changes every day. The world is changing, and I believe what we teach our child needs to change to match this.

So you want to teach your child to code? Start laying the foundation by slowly introducing some of these basic coding concepts to children, such as breaking down instructions, giving instructions in a methodical way, giving directions, deciphering codes, recognizing, and developing patterns.

Many children are kinetic learners and retain information far easier if they have hands-on experience with concepts, therefore, offline games are very important even if to us, as adults, they seem basic and far removed from the idea we envision when we think of computer coding.

These offline coding activities can be added into everyday routines. At home, you can just be playing fun activities with your child. The idea of the offline games is not only to get children away from the computer to teach the basic concepts but also to get them to think logically, learn to problem solve, work collaboratively as well as to learn patience, determination, and resilience. All skills that are valuable throughout life, not just for coding, can be learned through these fun games. Games such as mazes, treasure hunts, deciphering codes, sequencing pictures, and events, and writing instructions can all help with these important skills.

Once your child is ready to code on a computer, then look at different resources. I would always recommend going for free websites such as Scratch to learn block-based coding before moving on to paid subscriptions as you can find out if your child has an interest in them or not. Sometimes in a home environment, children prefer toys and apps over one specific website, so it may be worth looking Into these rather than a website subscription.

Remember, however, – and wherever – you are teaching, foster a good learning environment. Trial and error is all part of learning when it comes to coding. Children like it when adults make mistakes, so when you know that they have a good understanding of what you are teaching them, then you can make mistakes too. Does your child notice this and pick up on it?

If you are working at home with your child, then work together rather than leaving them to play by themselves. If possible, involve other family members, too. Coding doesn't have to be a boring, dry, academic subject. Foster that creativity in your children by being creative yourself. Have fun and enjoy bonding with your child!

Made in the USA
Monee, IL
17 November 2020